Pursue The Passion

Edited & Written By

BRETT FARMILOE

Photos By

JAY WHITING
NOAH POLLOCK
ZACH HUBBELL
BRETT FARMILOE

Design By

KRISTEN ZIRKLER

College grads traveling acr
to mee   te professi

2007 TOUR SCHEDULE

www.pursueth

Find Out More

ne country
who
their jobs
Pursue The Passion
on.com
Tour Sponsored By
Jobing.com

Pursue The Passion

Published By People Department Publishing
4747 N 22nd St, Phoenix AZ 85016

RTH DAKOTA
MINNESOTA
TH DAKOTA
WISCONSIN
MICHIGAN
NEW YORK
PENNSYLVANIA
IOWA
NEBRASKA
ILLINOIS
INDIANA
OHIO
W. VIRGINIA
VIRGINA
KENTUCKY
NSAS
MISSOURI
NORTH CAROLINA
TENNESEE
OKLAHOMA
ARKANSAS
SOUTH CAROLINA
ALABAMA
GEORGIA
MISSISSIPPI
TEXAS
LOUISIANA
FLORIDA

To: Anyone who feels corralled down a beaten path

Lake Oswego, OR

254-56 DAUPHINE ST
MOBILE, AL 36602

CHICAGO IL 606
PH.# (773) 871-1

KEYSTONE SD 57751
605-666-4654

6404 Mission Gorge
San Diego, CA 92120

THANK YOU FOR
SHOPPING BIG EASY
TRAVEL PLAZA
5000 OLD GENTILLY RD
NEW ORLEANS, LA
1-504-943-5000

WELCOME TO
QUICKWAY #61
RT 49 & INT 81
CENTRAL SQUARE NY

WELCOME
777 CASINO CENTER DRIVE
BILOXI
MS

DIAMOND SHAMROCK
2416 NORTH MAIN
JUNCTION, TEXAS

7-11 #57636
6500 ESCONDIDO
EL PASO   TX
Station: 636

SHELL
9260 S EASTERN
LAS VEGAS   NV 89123

EXXON EXPRESS PAY

WALL AUTO LIVERY
SD   577900000
DLR#   9498872

INTERSTATE CHEVR
7501 WASHINGTON AVE.
OCEAN SPRINGS MS 39564
228-872-1955

NEW YORK STATE
THRUWAY AUTHORITY

JIF-E MART #4
TRAVEL SHOP
MADISONVILLE, TX.

Coxco @ CasaBlanca
5960 N. Oracle Rd.
Tucson, Arizona

WELCOME TO
ROTTEN ROBBIE
1006180434-001
55 E.TODD ROAD

ROTTEN ROBBIE #60
SANTA ROSA CA

HILLTOP SPIRIT
722 E. Cypress
Redding, CA 960

NEWTON 128 MOBIL
RT. 128 SOUTH
NEWTON, MA 02452

WELCOME TO
HIGHLAND MARKET
MEMPHIS TN 38111

FIVE STAR C-STORE
2301 RIVERSIDE DRI
NASHVILLE   TN
R# 00033215013

WELCOME TO
VALERO
WYANDOT PLAZA
GENOA, OH

167 Beale St
Memphis, TN 38103
(901) 529-1544

WELCOME TO
OUR STOP

Dateland Exxon
H.M.P. 67
Dateland AZ 85333

C&C ARCO
7202 S 320th St.
Federal Way, WA

Scottsville Plaza
WestHenrietta NY14586
Thank You
For Your Business

Lake Plaza Chevron
Cumming, Ga
N 00?? 105

TEXACO 0005365
SOUTH TOWN EXPRESS
25 EAST 1100 SOUTH
RICHFIELD   UT

Welcome to
Hy-Vee Gas
2717 Bridge Avenue
Albert Lea MN 560
507-377-2952

BP Connect
Romeoville   IL

PRICE/GAL $2.799

BROOKSHIRE AMOCO
3521 BROOKSHIRE
CHARLOTTE, NC 28216

921 Pearl Street
Boulder, Colorado
80302
(303) 444.4888

236 MASS AVE NE
WASHINGTON DC 20002

FastPay

THANK YOU!

PUMP# 6
SHELL
448 HARTFORD TURNPIK
VERNON CT

26.795G
1009 S SPLITROCK
BRANDON
BLVD
SD

7693500-01

COFFEE CUP FUEL

LakelandPlaza Chevron
502 Lakeland Plaza
Cumming, Ga

GRAVIER'S CHEVRON
44801 HWY. 101
LAYTONVILLE, CA.

SHELL
1101 MONTEREY
SAN LUIS OBIS CA

LUCYS SAN MARCOS
141 E HOPKINS
SAN MARCOS TX 78666
512-558-7399

1663
TX 77665
-4422

752 N.HIGHLAND
ATLANTA, GA 30306

ARCO am/pm PSI#5499
242 NE Terry Lane
Grants Pass, OR 975

MINI MART INDIANA TOLL RD 7S
HOWE, IN 46746

14940
LINNIE, TX
409
C

39880 E. Hwy 80
Tacna, AZ

HRCO #4358
PSI #5236
14650 Bel-Red Rd.
Bellvue, WA 98007

Thriftway #2
1900 S Montana
BUTTE MT 59701

501 N HIGGINS AVE
MISSOULA, MONTANA
59802
406-728-8888

SHELL
701 E DICKINSON BLVD
FORT STOCKTON TX

WELCOME

SALES RECEIPT
#7 424 360504
SHELL
176 N MATHILDA AVE
SUNNYVALE   CA 94085

116TH T GROCERY
3628 116TH AVE NE
MARYSVILLE, WA.

MOBIL ON-THE-RUN
1401 SOUTH FIFTH ST
ST. CHARLES, MO 63

Welcome
Walden Gas Mart #131
I-55 S. @ Hwy 35.
Walden, MS 39176
662-464-5914
WALDEN GAS MAR

ARCO #24335
1310 4th St.
Santa Rosa Ca. 95404

PUMP# 12
Store #1290
1318 Main Street
Lordsburg, NM

WELCOME TO

1505 BUS. HWY. 18-151E
MT. HOREB, WI 53572

Shopping at Circle
Tucson, AZ 85719
520-622-5290

76/CIRCLE K #556
2022 S PUGET DR
RENTON, WA 98055000

GREAT BRIDGE SERVICENTER
208 S. BATTLEFIELD BLVD
CHESAPEAKE, VA. 23322
757-482-2075

1399 Robson Street
Vancouver, BC, V6E1C6

LOCO FOOD STORE
722 HORIZON DRIVE
GRAND JCT, COLORADO

Laguna Tool
124 N. Coast Hwy
Laguna Beach

CHEVRON PLAZA
CUMMING GA 30400

WELCOME
CAR-MAC SHELL
HOLLAND, MO.

226 SW Broadway
Portland, OR 97205
(503) 241 3488

Vons Gas
1680 Garnet Ave
Pacific Beach, CA,
92109
STORE NO: 2116

P.O. Box 1   52551 Ash Road
Granger, IN 46530
Tel. (574)674-9836

ARCO am/pm FAC#06501
15320 NW Cornell Rd
Beaverton, OR 97006
Store: 06501

MR. DISCOUNT GAS
1285 E ENNIS AVE
ENNIS TEXAS

139 E 54 St
NEW YORK NY 10016
212-213-117

251 Lincoln Blvd
Venice, Ca 90291

631 State Street
Madison, WI 5370
251-8908

Mellow Mushroom
Keep on Shroomin'
2426 Guadalupe St
Austin, TX 78705

Part I: The Pursuit

Denver, CO

One summer, a couple buddies and I decided to hit the road. We were graduating from college and had no idea what we wanted to do with our lives. The solution to our 'what should I do with my life' dilemma was to travel around the country and interview people who had jobs they loved. We hoped their insight and advice would help us find our way.

We started scheduling interviews, planning our route, and lining up places to stay. I spent the last of my savings on an RV I bought off of Craigslist and named her Maggie Miracles. Two days after walking across stage in a cap and gown, we packed up the RV and headed out for what surely would be the adventure of our lives.

The journey began with us interviewing the namesake of our business college, our coveted college basketball coach, and a larger than life car salesman. Then, three hours into the trip, we broke down. Green liquid discharged onto the pavement. Steam spewed from under the hood. It sounded like a bag of marbles let loose when we tried to start the engine.

Needless to say, the question of 'what should I do with my life' was left unanswered. We scrapped the tour we planned, and quietly lived out the remainder of the summer before going our separate ways into the working world. My destination? Corporate auditing.

There's a statistic I read not too far into my first job. It said more than half of the American workforce is unhappy with their work. That's more than 75 million Americans who dislike what they do for a living. That's sad and significant. As I fulfilled my duties as a corporate auditor, I found myself among the millions of people who wake up every morning dreading the day ahead.

What I learned from the experience is that the goal, for any of us, should be to love our work. It's not possible to love your job every second of every day, but the idea is that work doesn't always have to suck. If we look at that statistic of half the workforce not liking their job, that means there's still plenty of people who are passionate about their career.

My question was, what are the people who enjoy their work doing that the people who dislike their job aren't doing?

HONK if you LOVE YOUR JOB

Phoenix, AZ

I quit my job to figure out the answer to that question. I created a website, started planning another tour, and recruited a few friends to help actively search for sponsors to fund our project.

At first, we thought we could get on a reality show. We took Maggie Miracles, our dysfunctional RV, out of storage and drove to Los Angeles. The first thing that happened when we got to LA was the awning fell off. Avoiding the Los Angeles traffic, we scooped up the awning, duct taped it to the top of the roof, and minutes later pulled into the audition parking lot for MTV's show *Pimp My Ride*.

Throughout the day, people dropped by and heard about what we would do if we got our ride pimped. Crew and cast members from the show stopped by and pumped us up with grandiose plans of putting a hot tub on the roof and flatscreens throughout the cabin. Then the moment of truth came: the producer dropped by.

The producer entered the RV with more of a watchful eye. He looked at the 80's style drapery, the antiquated antennae televisions, and asked the tough questions like, 'Does this thing work?' Then his eyes fixated on something in the back of the RV.

"You guys go to U of A?" he asked, referring to the large, red and blue University of Arizona flag we had proudly hung above our beds.

"Hell yeah! Bear Down!" we said, trying to come across as overly enthusiastic to better our chances at being on the show.

"That sucks" the producer said. "Because I went to Arizona State. You guys have a good ride home."

The producer walked out of the RV, the crew members shrugged their shoulders, and we had received our first rejection to sponsor Pursue the Passion. **It wouldn't be our last.**

When we were voted off the parking lot, we pitched every kind of corporation you can imagine. We pitched family and friends. We made a proposal to our business school. We picked up a phone book and dialed random businesses. We signed with an agent and tried to get a book deal. We begged frat houses to let us stay with them. We wrote so many blind emails that our outgoing messages started to get flagged as spam.

We were rejected, hung up on, ignored, and escorted out of places more times than I'd like to mention.

Potential Sponsor List	Yes	Result	No
MTV Pimp My Ride	☐		☑
Eller College of Management	☐		☑
Red Bull	☐		☑
Chevron	☐		☑
Shell	☐		☑
Deloitte.	☐		☑
Toyota	☐		☑
Cruise America	☐		☑
Applebee's	☐		☑
Dove Chocolate	☐		☑
Hilton	☐		☑
Perkins Coie	☐		☑
Inc 500	☐		☑
Young $ Magazine	☐		☑
Blue Media	☐		☑
University of Arizona	☐		☑
IBM	☐		☑
Wells Fargo	☐		☑
Socko	☐		☑
KOA	☐		☑
Logan's Roadhouse	☐		☑
StartupNation.com	☐		☑
Gönink Design & Print	☐		☑
Bear Naked	☐		☑
Price Waterhouse	☐		☑
Random House	☐		☑
ΣΦΕ	☐		☑
Mom & Dad	☑		☑

We did have one small success story before finding our breakthrough.

The situation was both a blessing and a curse. We received a sponsorship from a food company that sells frozen meals. The company gave us 200 coupons to be redeemed for a frozen pizza, a frozen burrito, or a frozen meal. In an effort to save money, we used these coupons for breakfast, lunch, and dinner for 30 days straight. If you've seen the movie *Super Size Me*, where the guy eats McDonald's for 30 days, our experience was exactly like that. After the 30th day, we vowed to never look at a frozen meal again.

A week after our frozen food diet detox, we began to think a little more clearly. **My friend Jay, who had been there through the whole sponsorship search, suggested I contact Jobing.com.** They were a local job board who had these funky wrapped cars, and were headquartered a block from our apartment. We figured we might be able to get them to sponsor a car wrap.

I wrote Jobing.com a blind email and ended up meeting with two of their Vice Presidents. Next thing I know I have an email in my inbox from Aaron Matos, the CEO of Jobing.com. He wanted to meet to talk about the idea and concluded the email by saying, 'Bring your big dreams.'

When I met Aaron I told him what we wanted to do. I'm sure that when I told him I'd like to have Jobing.com sponsor four guys to go across the country in an RV, he had a few flashbacks of the movie *Borat*. But after a pair of intense meetings, Jobing.com agreed to sponsor us because what we wanted to do aligned with their mission to help people improve their lives through the jobs they work.

Our world was flipped upside down with that sponsorship. Instead of traveling in an RV likely to break down, we were able to buy a fully functional RV with a custom car wrap. We weren't exactly able to eat lobster and steak, but a $20 a day budget allowed us to eat something other than frozen meals.

Most importantly, that sponsorship enabled us to embark on the journey of a lifetime.

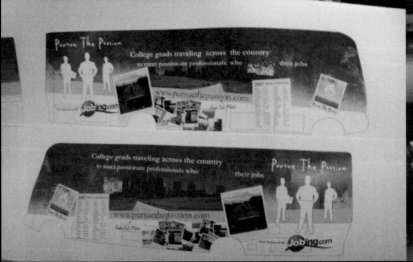

Phoenix, AZ

Jobing.co

College grads traveling across the country
to meet passionate professionals who   their jobs   Pursue The Pa

www.pursuethepassion.com

17

Brett

I was an optimistic entrepreneur without experience when embarking on the tour. After years of studying and working in accounting, I was in desperate need of something real, exciting, and alive. Pursue the Passion was the answer that I was searching for.

Usually when you pack, you always forget one thing. But I don't think I forgot anything. I hit the road with a PC, paper, pens, ironed shirts, and dreams.

Jay

Jay Whiting (aka J. Foxx) was a Communications major with a few months remaining at the University of Arizona. His immediate plans after graduation were to travel around the country to promote the music from his group, Class Project, and their first album entitled Rough Draft. We had met in my first campus visit to the UofA, and had remained friends throughout college.

Knowing that Jay was looking to take his show on the road, I believed that we could blend the Class Project and Pursue the Passion tours together. I drove down to Tucson to meet with Jay, and we agreed to merge the tours. He humbly accepted my couch as a temporary home, and a $6 hour wage to help with the sponsorship search.

Jay was there for the *Pimp My Ride* rejection, the *Super Size Me* experiment gone wrong, and the Jobing.com sponsorship. He hit the road with a camera to capture interview footage, a Mac to edit video, and boxes full of Class Project CD's to distribute across the country.

# of us in the RV.

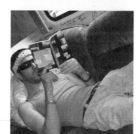

Noah

Noah Pollock (aka Knomad) was a Spanish Linguistics and Creative Writing major at the University of Arizona. Noah and Jay had been hallmates in the dorms, and united their talents to form the group Class Project. I had lived with Noah my junior year. Also joining us in that living situation was our best friend Dan, and a randomly assigned roommate. Her name was Shannon, and she held an occupation my Mom did not approve of.

The LSAT and the prospect of law school weighed heavily on Noah's mind as graduation came and went. The tour pulled him in a different direction. Noah hit the road with an older Mac laptop in which he would write summaries of the interviews, read the New York Times, and update his Facebook status.

Zach

Zach Hubbell was an unhappy auditor who spent the majority of his days auditing Indian reservations in the middle of nowhere Arizona. When he wasn't on the road for work, he was living in a loft in my one bedroom apartment. We had known each other from accounting classes, and decided to live together when we made the move from Tucson to Phoenix.

The day we got the sponsorship, Jay and I decided to ask Zach to come with us. When we got home from test driving RV's, we found Zach mopping around in the kitchen, exhausted from another week of work. I went up to him and said, 'Zach, I know something you don't know.' He said, 'What's that?' I said, 'On Monday morning, you're going to walk in to your office and you're going to quit your job. You're coming on the Pursue the Passion tour with us.'

Zach spent a weekend pondering the possibilities. On Monday, he quit his job. A couple weeks later, the four of us hit the road. Zach forgot to pack a pillow and a blanket.

In total we traveled 16,000 miles in 38 states, and were on the road for 120 days.

The trip took us to over 50 generous host families; including (but not limited to) the welcoming home of my stepdad's great aunt Pinky in Seattle, my friend's friend's ex-girlfriend's friend's house in Nashville, and the apartment of a deaf Wall Street broker who was pursuing other dreams in Akron.

The RV went through well known cities like New York, Los Angeles, Chicago; landmarks like Mount Rushmore, the Capitol, the Golden Gate Bridge; natural wonders like the Redwood Forest, Old Faithful, Niagara Falls; and to lesser known towns like Lusk, Burt, and Dawsonville.

Most importantly, we interviewed people who loved what they did for a living. The interviews took us to large companies like Microsoft, Nike, and the *New York Times*. We were welcomed to personal spaces like living rooms, favorite coffee spots, and tour buses. We found ourselves in odd places like a goat farm, a mechanics parking lot, and a prison. We interviewed people with occupations ranging from a doctor, lawyer, and an accountant to a shoe designer, a yoga master, and a janitor. In all, we talked with more than 250 people who had pursued their passion.

How did these people get to where they are today?
What did each of them have in common? From their advice, life
stories, regrets, highlights and personal pursuits, we've found three things that each interviewee had in common when it came to their pursuit.

ORAL HISTORIAN

You think you don't have control over your life?
Walk out your front door, turn left, keep going,
keep going, keep going, don't look back, keep
going...you're free.

You can change your entire life.
Just like that.

ORAL HISTORIAN
I think what I do is something
anybody can try. It's not that
daunting. I started out with
no experience. Just a passion
for wanting to meet girls and
go to concerts for free.

*Roll the Credits: **P207***

Ownership

Ownership is the decision
to dictate our environment through our actions.

It's much easier to let our environment dictate what we do. It's much easier to abide by social norms and reach goals by observing specific protocols. It's much harder to decide you want something and to go after it by blazing your own path. Ownership is that point where you say, 'This is what I'm going to do.'

It was during my last on campus interview when I decided that Pursue the Passion was an idea worth pursuing. I had gone through about 20 interviews the fall semester of my senior year with various recruiters and senior managers. What I found in the recruiting process is that I really enjoyed turning the table around and asking the interviewer questions about their job. I remember spacing out in my last interview and thinking, 'This can't be my last interview. I've got to continue this.'

That night I went home and took some ownership on the idea. I whipped out a pencil and some scratch paper and wrote down what I wanted to accomplish before going into the working world. I wanted to explore what else was out there. I wanted to interview people about how they found their passion. I wanted to provide information to students like me who needed some real guidance and direction. And I wanted to travel.

At my desk that night, the idea for Pursue the Passion was born and plans were put in motion.

Taking ownership is hard because we construct so many imaginary barriers around what we can or can't do. We think that we're not pretty enough, talented enough, or smart enough. We are never completely positive if it's the right decision. We're not sure on how to go about pursuing an idea. Whatever the barrier may be, taking ownership is difficult because there are a lot of gray areas that permit us from taking action.

The news is that no one is going to give you what you want if you don't go after it. Many of our interviewees grappled with difficult questions when deciding on whether or not to pursue an idea. But the fact is, every person we interviewed, at one point or another, had to take ownership to begin their pursuit.

COLLEGE STUDENT Personally, I'm procrastinating on making a decision. Hopefully it's a little bit different with other people. It's just that there are a lot of options you can do. If I want to be a lawyer, I better start preparing by focusing on studying for the LSAT. If I'm going to be a doctor, I better starting studying for the MCAT.

The problem is that you don't really know what you want to do until you're actually doing it. So how do you know what you actually want until you get it and you try it? That's the big question. It's a big dilemma. But right now I have a lab class and gotta run.

MARKETING CONSULTANT I was unemployed and listless looking for my next move. And so, I went on a long road trip. At about North Carolina, it was cooking at a hundred degrees. I was sacked out on my friend's plastic sofa. And I said, 'What do I want to do with my life? What do I really, really want to do with my life?'

LIFE COACH There's so much anxiety around what you're going to do. **But it's not 'What should I do with my life?' It's 'What should I do next?**

PR FIRM PARTNER I wasn't too concerned about being successful or where I would end up. I was more short term focused in terms of 'Let's find something that I liked to do.' There were no expectations there either in terms of starting the firm and making it successful or not successful. We basically said, 'Let's give this six months and see what happens.'

PARK RANGER If you wanna do sumthin' just do it. Don't complain about it. Just do it. That's my opinion. No excuses.

I-25, Wyoming

FOOTWEAR DESIGNER By the time my senior year in high school came, I wanted to be a designer. So I started talking to my guidance counselor. I was telling her what I wanted to do. She's like, 'Well, you have a better chance at just going to the Army. Military is a much better choice for a young black kid who grew up in Inglewood than trying to be an artist because it just won't happen.'

That didn't sit well with me. I thought it was horrible advice to give a young kid. So I started looking in the newspaper for jobs in design. I found this really small, one fourth inch by one inch ad that Reebok had for a freelance footwear design contest. So I entered it, and I won the contest. I was 17 years old. But Reebok didn't hire me because I was only 17. They thought I went to design school. They told me to come back once I graduated from school and then maybe they'd give me a job.

I kept having all these roadblocks along the way. At one point, I started to get seriously discouraged. I couldn't talk to anyone that was actually in the field. There were no schools that could teach footwear design. It was just discouraging.

I started working part time at this accounting agency called Account-Temps. Me and my best friend signed up at the same time. His job assignment was LA Gear, but he couldn't find it. The manager got upset with him and sent me. So the next day I went and I found it and started working at LA Gear as a file clerk.

When I got there, they were changing over management and leadership. The new management wanted to find out more about the company. They solicited the employees on ways to make the company better and find ways to improve it. For me, my suggestion was to hire me as a footwear designer. Every day, for six months, I put my shoe sketches in the suggestion box.

One day the owner of the company called me into his office. He thought I went to school. He thought I graduated from college in design. I was like, 'I'm just a file clerk. As a matter of fact, I'm a temp. I don't even work here full time.' He was like, 'Well, you want a job?'

So in January of 1989, I got my first official footwear design job. I was an entry level footwear designer for LA Gear.

Ownership

CONSERVATIONIST I was hired by a company called Financial Coordinators. They offered me an amazing salary for that time. A company car, which was a big deal. A nice expense account and a lot of security. I went back to my third and fourth interview and I looked at my new office and met the people working there, all a little bit older than me, and thought that I had tremendous opportunity.

Two days later, a friend of mine was being interviewed at this place called Africa USA. They raise wild animals there. I went along with him, and while he was being interviewed, I was looking around at people bottle feeding lion cubs and tiger cubs. I saw a fella walking a zebra on a leash. I saw a giraffe go by.

I thought this is amazing!

So I went to interview for the job myself, just for the fun of it. Well, they called me the next day and offered me the job. I talked to this fella on the phone for hours and hours. If I can step backwards a few years, as a child, my grandfather was a forester. My entire childhood was in wildlife, and in wild places. It just clicked.

I'll never forget the night of my welcome aboard party at Financial Coordinators. I called them and said,

'I decided I'm not going to be taking your job.'

They were a little angry and said, 'Why not! Is it another company? Have they offered you more? We'll meet their offer!' I said, Actually no. They've offered me less. I'm going to make less money and work more hours.

But it's a job I think I'm going to love.

CELEBRITY CHEF I would say that it's a really bad idea to sit around and say, "Yeah, I haven't really figured out what I want to do." My advice is to put on a costume of some kind and pick something, and be it.

And if it doesn't work out, take the costume off, pick something else that seems closer to what you love, and be that. Just practice actually being one thing instead of…contemplating. And not doing.

BARTENDER I've realized what's important. It's not money. It's not what you have. It's what you have inside of you. It's about connecting your brain to your heart. Twelve inches from greatness. My dad always told me that. I think that's a line we have to live with.

ANIMATOR When I was younger, my mom and dad would tell me that I had to find something else to do. They'd say, "It's cool that you like to draw and that you're good, but you're not going to make a living at it so you better find something else to do." My dad was a business guy. He could not get me at all. He was just like, 'You are one weird kid.'

But I didn't know any better. I went to them and said, 'You know, if I could do this, I don't want to do anything else. I can't think of anything else that I'd want to do. I'm not a salesman or a lawyer. I don't want to do anything else. If I can't be an animator or a cartoonist, I don't know what I'll do. I'll just do whatever and make the most money I could make or whatever because I'm not going to be enjoying anything.' I just couldn't get that out of my head that animation was what I wanted to do.

I moved down to LA with absolutely no prospects at all. I started working on my portfolio to try and get into Disney. This guy said it was going to take me three or four tries to get into Disney because they weren't going to accept me the first time I applied.

I said, 'Ok, whatever.' I did a bunch of drawings for months. I'd go to the park every day, or the zoo. Every day. I'd just draw, draw, draw whatever I saw. I applied at Disney, and they called me back. I'm like, 'Whoa.'

I didn't expect to start right away, but that's how it began. I was there for all those years during *Little Mermaid, Aladdin*, all those movies. So if you really want to do it, it's one of those deals where no one can talk you out of it. You really just have to believe in it.

South Bend, IN

MARKETING CONSULTANT If you have great abilities and passion, you end up with this great intersection. Why would you not be successful? It's hard not to be successful. You have the talent. You have the skills. You have the things that you need. But you also have the passion in that same area. So pursue that.

ACCOUNTING PROFESSOR When you are deciding where to work, you are told it is a life decision, but it's not. You're young and if you don't like what you're doing then you can get out of the situation and still be 24 and have your entire life ahead of you.

CHEMICAL ENGINEER I didn't plan on going back to school. I always wanted to, but I didn't think that was going to happen. It wasn't until I think I realized that my work was dangerous, where you're on the road at night, and you work weekends, and you don't go home right away…so I finally said, 'Forget it. I'm going to quit and go back to school.'

That was very scary. I'm 32 years old and was talking to my wife about how I could start the process. I laugh now about it because I told my friends from high school about my decision to go back and pursue engineering. They were like, 'Yeah right. And I'm going to fly to the moon.'

ASTROLOGER What's comfortable and what's fulfilling are opposites to me. Sitting on the couch eating ice cream and watching movies is comfortable. That gets old after a couple of days. You have to get up and stretch. That desire to get up and stretch is your calling. That's calling you to do something that's as far away from that comfort zone and takes the most energy to actually go out and do.

Every time you are called to do something and you follow it, you're following what you're supposed to be learning in this lifetime. That makes for a certain sense of fulfillment.

TASTEMASTER When I was looking for a job, I got on the internet, Jobing.com, all those ones that you go on to look for a job. When this job came up, I not only applied on the internet, but I emailed my resume in. I sent it by snail mail. I faxed it in. I went down Monday morning with a shirt and tie shoving my resume in their face saying I'm your guy! I'm your guy! Let me talk to somebody!

I even called the general number, and at that time you could press 5 and get the CEO of the company. Which I did. 'Hello Mr. CEO, you don't know me but I've been applying now for two days for this job in R&D for ice cream. I'm your guy.' I left him a message, I left the chairman of the board a message. Didn't know these guys at all. But again, I wasn't afraid to stick my neck out and tell them that I'm your guy and I've got the skills and that I was a perfect for it.

I hit them from every angle because I felt that I was the guy for the job. I was so passionate about trying to get the job that they couldn't help but give it to me.

Crescent City, CA

RESTAURANT MANAGER I came to the back door. I pounded on the back door. I didn't have an interview. I was a punk back in the day. I said, "Let me in here, and let me work for two weeks. You can pay me when you think I'm good enough to get paid."

Whatever it takes to get in the door, and I just did that. I started at the bottom. The lowest spot. And I just powered my way through by working as hard as I could. You start at the bottom and you realize what the bottom is. It's more of a great foundation.

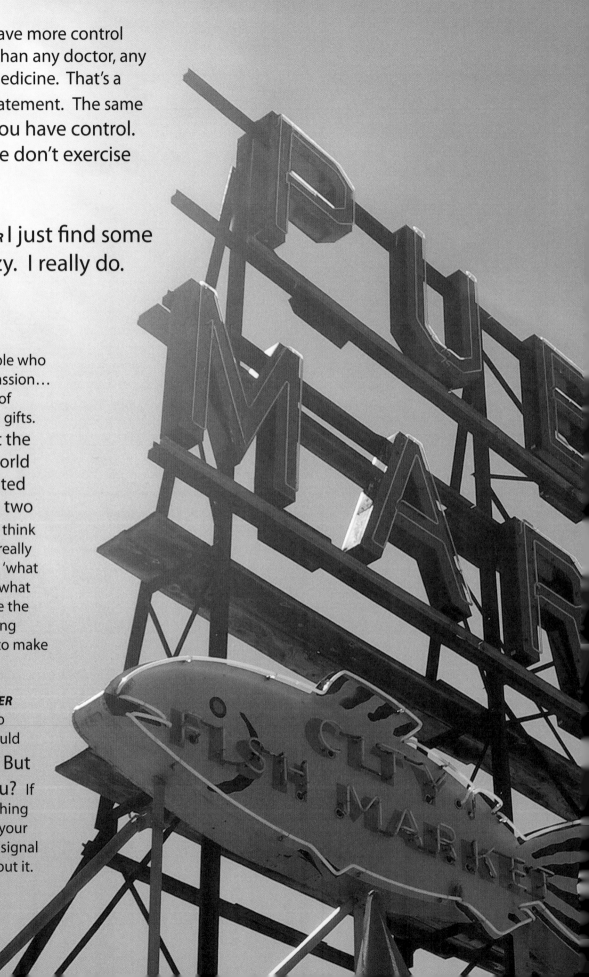

Ownership

NUTRITIONIST You have more control over your health than any doctor, any hospital, or any medicine. That's a really powerful statement. The same is true with life. You have control. But most people don't exercise that control.

VIDEO GAME DESIGNER I just find some people are lazy. I really do.

SOCIAL ACTIVIST People who are pursuing their passion… it's not just a matter of discerning their own gifts. It's also looking at the suffering of the world and being motivated to combine those two things together. I think that's what we're all really called to do. We ask, 'what are my gifts?' Then, 'what suffering touches me the most?' Then, you bring those two together to make a difference.

POUND CAKE PRODUCER What you love is a no brainer, and you should go in that direction. But what irritates you? If you don't like something and it really gets on your nerves, then that's a signal to do something about it.

CEO I grew up in Egypt, a very rich country from a tourism standpoint. In my neighborhood, there were a lot of tourists from all over the world. I was one of those people that could speak Italian, English, French…so at a very young age, I really had an idea that I wanted to be a part of tourism. But I didn't know how.

At age 16 I decided to travel on my own. At the time it was less than $100 bucks to get a roundtrip from Cairo to Paris. That was literally all the money I had. As soon as I landed at the airport I started asking people if they would give me a job. Finally, a restaurant took me in. I fell in love with that business. That was my first job in tourism.

In my case, I really followed something that was as simple as speaking languages. But in order for me to speak languages, I really had to be around people from different parts of the world. And in order to be around people from different parts of the world, I had to be in tourism. It was as simple as that.

33

Seattle, WA

New Orleans, LA

Occidental, CA

Mobile, AL

DISASTER VOLUNTEER I was here during Katrina. I was in the Superdome. Matter fact, I had two weeks to graduate culinary school before Katrina hit. The house I was living in, this lady just up and sold my house. So I had to find somewhere to go. I decided to go volunteer.

I started off cleaning up grounds. I was working in the area across the bridge in the Upper 9th. There were some cooks there that didn't care about the food. They'd just throw some stuff together and you'd put it in your mouth and you'd be like, 'What the hell?' You'd be like, 'I know what this is, but it don't taste like it should taste.' I cook too good to be eating like that.

People came here to help the people in New Orleans. I appreciate them coming to help. But they gotta eat! The stuff I started eating when I first came here I wouldn't want anybody to eat that. I seen where they needed help. So I stepped up and just took cooking for the volunteers on full time. Since then, I cook maybe 300-400 plates a week by myself from scratch.

There's a lot of good people that need to be fed. They just trying to help too. So now I'm out feeding everyone and contributing where I can best contribute.

HIGH SCHOOL PRINCIPAL I was frustrated as a teacher that I didn't get the help I needed in the classroom. After teaching for many years, I thought, 'What's the roadblock that didn't allow me to help the students?' I felt that administratively, I could get in there and help better. I could make the right connections and help the students. That's why I decided to go into administration.

VIDEO GAME DESIGNER What I did was I got a copy of MVP '05. The last MVP game that came out. I played it, and I had a pad and paper next to me. As I played it, I wrote down the things that I didn't like and compressed it all together into a single page email of the top 10 things I would do to make the game better. I sent that to the producer of the game, and he basically offered me a job and said I want you on my team. When I wrote up that paper on MVP, I wasn't even an employee of EA Sports.

ANIMATOR As an animator, you have to come up with ideas. You don't just sit here and animate the way it's laid out and that's it. If you have a better idea to make it funnier, then you do that. You come up with ideas also. You don't just dig in like this is an assignment. You have to think about what the most entertaining way to get this across.

ENTREPRENEURSHIP EXPERT

Every great thing we have in the world started with an idea.

Phoenix, AZ

STOK

14K KGUE

Berkeley, CA

Chicago, IL

Ownership

BASKETBALL EXECUTIVE We were going to Denver for the 1984 All-Star game. Everyone in the league would come in on Saturday night and have a nice banquet, then they'd play the game on Sunday and go home. My idea was to turn the All-Star game into All-Star weekend with sponsorable events like a Slam Dunk contest and an old timers game.

I visited the commissioner to share my idea and he looked at me like I was crazy.

Thousand Oaks, CA

The weekend was the finale of his reign and he just wanted to go out nicely. He didn't want to be taking a lot of chances on his final weekend as commissioner. But he came around and told me that if it didn't cost the league any money and it wouldn't embarrass him, that I could try it.

I signed Gatorade as the sponsor of the slam dunk contest, and American Airlines paid for all the players who were coming in for the old timer's game. That was really the start of the sponsorship program for the NBA which has grown into something much bigger now.

Santa Rosa, CA

LIFE COACH I would say to just jump. Anytime you spend overanalyzing things, you're just wasting time. Anytime you're not making a decision, you are making a decision. Which is to do nothing.

Chicago, IL

YOUTH PROGRAM DIRECTOR I went to a public school in Chicago and they had great school programs. We were teaching in a school were they had no programs. So we wanted to do something for these kids because they didn't have any kind of way to get themselves involved.

We started playing soccer with a dozen kids before school. We had these kids just coming straight out the projects.

Within three weeks, we had 30-35 kids out there. That's when the teachers and the school administration and the school counsel president were just like 'wow.' They were totally amazed.

After that initial season where we were just doing it for fun, people approached us and said we should make it more a long term consistent program because the kids, the teachers, the families…everyone in the community loved it. The snowball effect is amazing. It has evolved into working with 200 students over six schools in four different communities, and is still going, which is really the most exciting thing about it.

ENTREPRENEURSHIP EXPERT There's always chances. There's always choices. There's always opportunities. I think that when things are going really badly, you try to look at the other choices. There's other directions that you can go. There's many businesses that started doing one thing, and they morph into doing something totally different.

One of the best parts about life is if you have a bad day, you go to bed at night, you wake up the next morning, you get another chance to succeed.

STAFFING FIRM CEO I watch that movie Sliding Doors with Gwyneth Paltrow. Did you ever see that? She makes that train, her life is completely different than if she doesn't make that train. Every decision you make will have lingering effects in your life. But you've got to make that choice.

BUS DRIVER I used to gang bang in St. Paul and sell drugs on the street corners. I was always in and out of prison. One day I was sitting on the corner selling and I was sick of it. I looked up at the sky and said, 'Lord, what can I do?'

Right then a Metro Transit bus pulled up next to me and let some passengers off. That moment was a real catalyst for me to escape the lifestyle I was in. I decided right then that I wanted to be a bus driver. I'm going on my tenth year now of driving buses for the city.

BOOK STORE MANAGER We can't find and explore our passion sitting on our couch watching Survivor. We can't always find it in the bar. But we can find it by engaging and stepping outside of our comfort zone. I think you find an interesting life if you do that.

DONATION ADVOCATE Aunt Patti had just gotten married. She was 34 years old. She was pregnant. They had just bought a house. It was the beginning of her life. And within a week, it was over. It just stunned me because I felt like…we are not guaranteed another day. You know? I can't be sitting in this basement doing a job that is so mundane and unsatisfactory, knowing that life has so much potential and I'm just letting it fly right by me.

So I quit that job. I took out loans. I went back to school. I got my English degree. I graduated in two years. I started making my way in the business world, much happier than I was ever before.

EXECUTIVE TV PRODUCER Look at what people have done before you, and do something completely different. If you look people who have 'made it' in my business, very, very few of them did this and this and this. They have all gone in their own direction.

You just take a path less traveled with skills and drive and passion you'll eventually get to where you want to go.

STAFFING FIRM CEO Where people get shifted is when they believe they have to do something. You think you got a degree for four years, and that this is the road I have to take. But it doesn't have to be like that.

GARDENER I had a life threatening blood disease that was pretty rare. That was when I was trying to make the transition into gardening. I thought that I may lose everything now. The doctor said, 'If the treatment doesn't work, you'll be gone in a year and a half.'

Well, my daughter is 10 years old. At that point I'm thinking, 'Wow. I don't have a choice. I've got to do this. If I don't try now, I will look back and I will say, 'You had this chance and you were just too afraid!'

DOCTOR Medicine was a career that the best and the brightest wanted. I was lucky because I approached it with a different angle. I had an accidental advantage. I majored in English but fulfilled all my pre med requirements. So I went in the small pile when it came to getting into medical school. That really gave me an advantage over all the other students because of the different approach, the different path that I took in college.

BASEBALL GM Sometimes you have a tendency to look at your peers and use them as a comparison or as a template for running your own business. We've tried to do the opposite.

We've tried to look at other industries and how they were doing things. We looked at guys like Warren Buffet and Berkshire Hathaway. We tried not to stay in our little box that we had here in baseball. We tried to look beyond and see where other people were drawing upon success.

YOGA MASTER To find it, whatever 'it' may be, requires a sense of letting go. And not being identified with all of the conditioning that society has given you as you were growing up. The conditioning comes from schooling and your parents and your church and media. All this…conditioning. I was going to say brainwashing. But I guess conditioning is probably a better word.

I-70, Colorado

COFFEE WHOLESALER In high school I was a mechanic. I worked on lawnmowers, chainsaws, that kind of thing. I was dirty every day of my life. It was a good job. Paid well for high school. I could go out on weekends, put gas in my car…the core essentials when you're 17 years old. But I was just tired of getting dirty.

My friend started a coffee business. He said if you're tired of being dirty every day, why don't you help us out? It's a lot of fun. You can sweep floors, fill orders, and just go from there. My parents, I remember my mom and dad saying I was crazy and I shouldn't do it. I had a decent paying job. It was steady. They told me not to go into coffee because it was risky and it was going to ruin paying for college and that kind of stuff.

We were 800 square feet in a fruit stand next to their dad's gas station. Eight and a half years later when I left that company we were 8,000 square feet, $15 million in sales a year.

My parents came full circle and actually invested their 401(k) in our company. My dad hated at least 15 years of work. He was like, 'If you guys can do something you enjoy, and not be where I was at after those 15 years, I'm all about supporting it.'

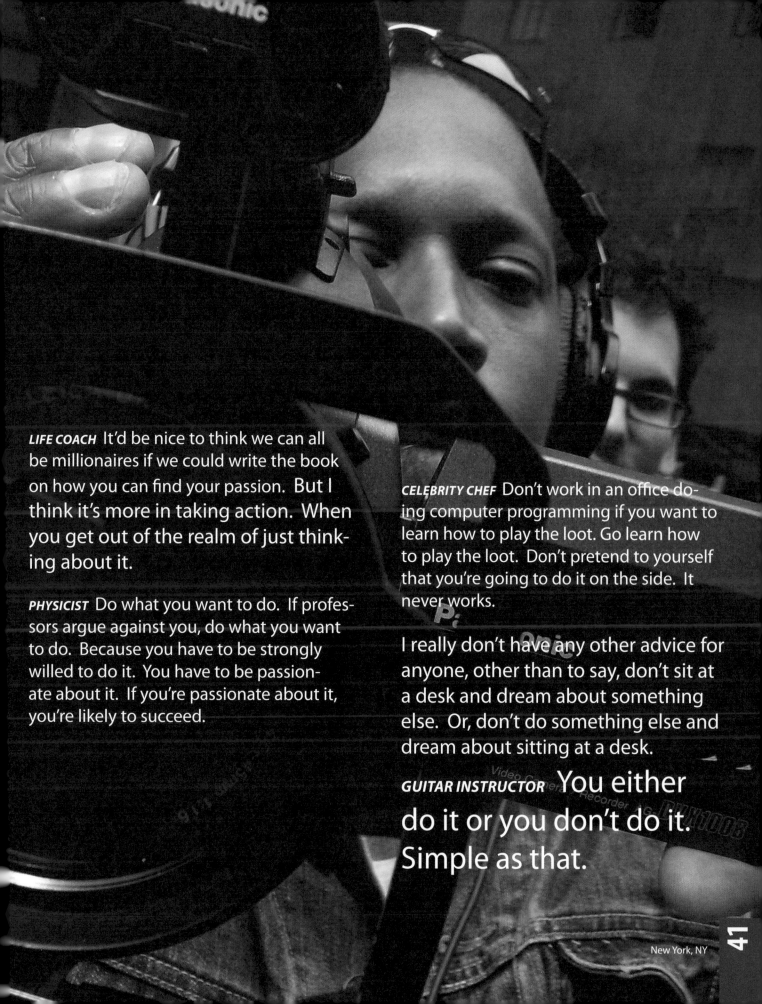

LIFE COACH It'd be nice to think we can all be millionaires if we could write the book on how you can find your passion. But I think it's more in taking action. When you get out of the realm of just thinking about it.

PHYSICIST Do what you want to do. If professors argue against you, do what you want to do. Because you have to be strongly willed to do it. You have to be passionate about it. If you're passionate about it, you're likely to succeed.

CELEBRITY CHEF Don't work in an office doing computer programming if you want to learn how to play the loot. Go learn how to play the loot. Don't pretend to yourself that you're going to do it on the side. It never works.

I really don't have any other advice for anyone, other than to say, don't sit at a desk and dream about something else. Or, don't do something else and dream about sitting at a desk.

GUITAR INSTRUCTOR You either do it or you don't do it. Simple as that.

New York, NY

You never know where the journey will lead you if you take ownership of it.

43

CELEBRITY CHEF

Dreams involve a lot of gambling.
Sometimes you win and you have a stack of chips.
Sometimes you look down and you have one little chip
looking back up at you.

CELEBRITY CHEF
Who cares if you're the clown,
as long as you dance in the
circus. That's pretty much the
attitude I've had about my line
of work my whole life. I could
have gotten a normal job. But
for some reason I decided to
jump in and take a chance at
something I wasn't good at.

Roll the Credits: P198

Risk

Taking a risk is when you have something to lose, but you decide to go all in anyway.

In every story that was shared with us, there came a point where a tough decision had to be made. Would they take a risk? Or would they decide it was too risky?

The risk that I took was quitting my job to do Pursue the Passion. When I walked into my boss's office to deliver the news, I was walking in with a guaranteed bi-monthly paycheck, benefits, social status, and a friend's resume to replace me. I knew that when I walked out of the office, I would have none of that.

I sat down in my boss's office with my friend's resume, now folded and soaked with sweat. Across from me sat my boss, smiling with an envelope in her hand.

"It looks like both of us have some news," she said. "Which one of us should go first?"

I volunteered. I told her about the reasons why I originally went into accounting (Job security. Good salary. Peer, parental, and professor pressure) and moved on to why I now wanted to leave accounting. What it came down to is that I could no longer stay in a job that I wasn't passionate about. By doing so, I'd be cheating myself, cheating the people around me, and cheating my employer. And most importantly, I felt I would never get to pursue what I really wanted if I didn't act now. I felt it would be a bigger risk to stay in accounting than to dive into the unknowns of Pursue the Passion.

"Do you want to know what's in the envelope?" my boss asked after accepting my friend's resume as my replacement. "It's a raise. Are you positive this is what you want to do?"

Most people turn away when there's risk involved. They take ownership, decide to do something, but when they get to that place where they have to take a leap, they don't jump.

Despite this, most of the people we talked to said that it was a bigger risk not to take a risk at all. Our interviewees saw the potential rewards being worth more than the potential loss. They identified what they were willing to risk and were clear on why they were risking it.

Taking a risk is a necessary step people take when in a pursuit.
Otherwise, you'll never get to the point where you want to be.

HOTEL MANAGER Everyone's a great general until wartime. Then you separate the leaders from whoever else there is.

MEDICAL CONSULTANT You have to believe when no body else does. Because you haven't shown anyone anything yet. So you have to believe it.

CARTOONIST There's a quote I read from this poet when I was in high school. It said that the risk to remain tight in the bud became greater than the risk it took to blossom. That mindset has been a part of me for this whole journey.

ENTREPRENEURSHIP EXPERT If you think about it from an economic standpoint, it makes absolutely no sense to start a business. If you look at the economic risk an entrepreneur takes, they're risking way too much for the return they might get.

I always talk about the statistics that 550,000 businesses every year get started in the United States, and 500,000 businesses go out of business every year in the United States. You have about a twenty percent chance of being in business after five years. So it is nuts!

The good part is that we don't measure it like that. Most people do it because they're passionate. Because they can help themselves. I say that I'm an entrepreneurholic, that I want to see my ideas succeed or fail. I don't have any choice but to go out and create these things. That's why we do it. We don't measure the risk.

Seattle, WA

HEDGE FUND MANAGER Whenever you make a big decision to do something very different, there's a push and a pull.

The push for me was I had gotten to a point in my career where I had scaled the peak and felt like I had accomplished all I was going to accomplish. It was really diminishing returns from there, both financially and physically. That was the push, it not being as fun as it was.

The pull was the dream. But you have to be willing to take risks to dream.

When I left Wall Street, here I am, married with two young children. I'm making a million dollars a year. And I'm saying, 'I'm going to walk away.'

I had people say to me, 'I wish I could do what you are doing.' Well, the reality is that they could have. But, one of the things you find is how risk averse people are. They say things to you like, "Well, how could you sell your house?" Well, because the dream is more important to me than living in a big house. I think one of the reasons why we don't dream is that we don't want to give up what we have currently.

Central Park, NY

If it's fixed, break it. That's our rule. No one else has that rule. They won't even go there because they're afraid at what might be inside. The more you do that, the greater the stuff that can happen.

Redwood Forest, CA

WRITER We had this team building activity and it was just me and this guy. Everything was completely confidential. He said, 'Your mind isn't here. What is going on with you?' I just melted. I started crying in front of him. You know when sometimes it hits you and your eyes get wet? I said, 'I just want to go write.' He said, 'You better make up your mind which hat you're going to wear. Because if you want it that much, you better go do it.'

At this point I was the number 2 person in a $500 million company. The company had paid a lot of money to recruit me in. They thought I came there to run the company. But I completely lost interest in what I was doing. My behavior didn't match my responsibilities. I couldn't live with the lack of integrity. I didn't think it was fair to the people who worked with me to mentally be somewhere else.

I went home to my husband and said that I wanted to quit and write full time. He was retired by then. It wasn't our financial plan at all. I was going to work another ten years. It wasn't that I hated my job, it was just that writing was what I wanted to do.

The company was flabbergasted when I left. When I quit, I thought, 'Oh my God. That phone's not going to ring.' But from the day I quit, I never missed that phone ringing. Ever. I didn't miss getting emails. I didn't miss presenting to thousands of people. I didn't miss having a nice office or a title or any of that crap. I didn't miss any of it. What was very important to me, and what made me happy, was not the same.

Yes, I was afraid. I mean there's nothing more risky...I don't know, what's risk? Financially it was extremely risky and is still. It doesn't make any sense. It's completely illogical what I did. Completely. But I'm much happier than I ever was, even when someone was paying me a lot of money. I can't explain it. But it's true. When there's personal satisfaction on the line, it's not a risk.

REAL ESTATE DEVELOPER When I was 25, I decided that I wanted to try and build houses. I was married, and I was a member of the grocers union when I decided to quit my job at Safeway. For a $10 fee I could keep my union status. My dad wanted me to pay the fee just in case something went wrong with my business. But I didn't pay it. For me, the option to return to the grocery store would always be in the back of my mind when business got tough. So I completely cut ties with my fallback option.

It was very risky. Because if that first house didn't sell…that first house was really important. But really, what do you have to lose? I mean, you're risking what you have. But when you're 22, you're not risking very much. I would say, especially when you're young, to take a risk.

I see kids your age and they're going to go in a profession that's a standard thing. My advice is to try something else first. For me it would be so much more fun to do your own thing and create something versus going to law school and going to work for a firm. It just seems like the bottom. It just seems like a death to me.

It's not a bad thing to do. I've got an older daughter who is 26. She's going to graduate school to get her PhD. I'm trying to talk her out of it. Friends are like, 'Why would you talk your daughter out of getting a PhD?' I tell them that the more you get into this pigeon-hole, the less you can do.

Most people like security I guess. But I wouldn't go for security when I was 22. There's plenty of time to get that. I'd say that whatever you want to do, really go after it. Take a risk. Do something different.

I mean, life is for an adventure. What kind of adventure do you want to have?

New York, NY

EXECUTIVE TV PRODUCER Right after graduation I went to work for this company that produced medical reports and sent it to radio and television stations all over the country. I got there and I was miserable. One of the guys I interned for on the *Today Show* called me right after I signed a contract with the company for a little bit more money. He said, 'I'm starting a production company in LA. You should come out and work for me.' He had no real job, no real nothing, but was like, 'Come work for me for free.'

I just did it. I broke my contract. I got sued. My buddy and I got in my car and drove to LA. I worked for two months for no money while I was trying different things doing production stuff. I got a job producing a news pilot show. Then I got

hired in the newsroom for the O.J. Simpson trial at KNBC.

Going to Los Angeles was probably the dumbest thing to do. You don't go to the biggest market and expect a job. But I lucked out. I showed up in LA and things happened. The other thing I would say that until you're 30, there's no such thing as 'taking chances.' There's no such thing. You can make mistakes and do things career wise that don't make sense and it doesn't matter. Because you're still learning.

SUSTAINABILITY ACTIVIST
So many people ask themselves, 'What if she won't go out with me?' What if. What if, what if! It's like putting energy in a knot. Let's see what happens when we put our energies into doing something, rather than putting our energies into not.

HEALTHCARE ENTREPRENEUR I find in my experience that entrepreneurs tend to embrace risk partly for the thrill of it. There is a thrill of doing something that hasn't been done before. And that something transcends normal patterns of rational behavior in many ways.

BOOK STORE MANAGER I had this advice from a very cool, radical grandmother about always taking this odd route. And I do think I ended up coming back to that advice.

I ended up buying what were former crack houses and turning them into art spaces.

What's interesting is that we put more money into fixing them up than the actual purchase price for the building. That got so popular that we opened a second arts collective down the street. And a third. We bought another building that the contractor said looked worse than Baghdad.

Taking a step back, I'm not a trust fund baby. The way I did it was in a very unconventional way. At the time, I was getting lots of credit card offers with zero down. I bought my first building by taking all the money off a credit card, and then refinancing the building six months later to pay back the credit card. I don't think that option exists anymore.

Now, First Fridays in downtown Phoenix are one of the largest art walks in the country. So the risk paid off.

Chicago, IL

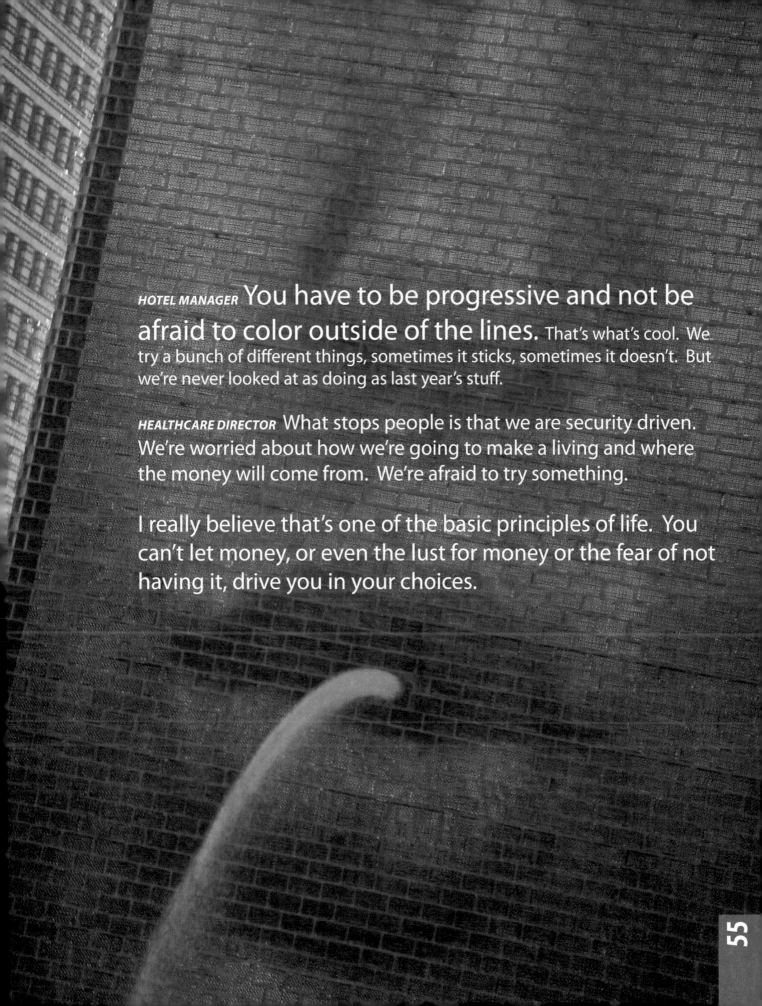

HOTEL MANAGER You have to be progressive and not be afraid to color outside of the lines. That's what's cool. We try a bunch of different things, sometimes it sticks, sometimes it doesn't. But we're never looked at as doing as last year's stuff.

HEALTHCARE DIRECTOR What stops people is that we are security driven. We're worried about how we're going to make a living and where the money will come from. We're afraid to try something.

I really believe that's one of the basic principles of life. You can't let money, or even the lust for money or the fear of not having it, drive you in your choices.

Mount Rushmore, SD

MARKETING CONSULTANT

What I've learned is that you're really not risking much if you don't lose focus of why you exist in the first place.

BOXING TRAINER I was told maybe thirty, forty years ago that if I wanted to make a lot of money in this sport, go to New York. I could have been introduced to people and wound up an instant millionaire for the experience I've had in boxing.

I talked to the family. My wife is from here. She's a twin. My kids liked it here. I thought life was more than the money and my family is more important than sacrificing what they want to do. If they're willing to stay with me, then I'll do what I'm doing and that's it. That's the decision I made.

BASEBALL GM There's two ways of looking at a career and life in general. If your pursuit is as much compensation as you can get right away, I think you're looking at things myopically.

If you're really good at something, people will find a way to pay you for it. Ultimately, you're going to be the best at that job if you're in a spot where you're not just professionally happy, but you're personally happy.

For me, I turned down the Boston Red Sox job. It was about four times the amount of money I was making. But, I would have only been taking it for two reasons.

One, to work for John Henry, who I have a lot of respect for, and ultimately because of the compensation. I realized that those weren't the right reasons to make a decision. As it's turned out, in the interim, I've recouped any lost compensation I would have had, and I have the opportunity to make more by virtue of making a decision for the right reasons.

ORAL HISTORIAN Eddie Murphy once told me that he didn't believe in having something to "fall back" on. Because if you're going to be a hairdresser while you're trying to be an actor, you'll end up being a hairdresser. So you really have to let go. After awhile you stop thinking about it. And you just do it.

CELEBRITY CHEF Be super broke and ridiculously broke for awhile and go right after what you love. Because you can't not practice your art. Even if it leaves you drinking dehydrated coffee and eating toast for a really long time. I ate a lot of toast.

Venice, CA

HEALTHCARE ENTREPRENEUR For us, it was terrifying financially to start our company. Only because we had families. Both of the founders had families and children that we were responsible for. From that perspective, it was terrifying at times. That created a great deal of stress. Not everyone has to go through that, especially those lucky enough to time things right. They don't have to do that bridge process themselves and put everything on the line.

But for us, it also got us through the hard times because we had everything on the line. We didn't have a choice. There was no backing out. That level of anxiety created the momentum to get us through the hard times, ironically.

SUSTAINABILITY ACTIVIST

Sometimes, there are a lot of changes of underwear when undertaking something like this.

NAME TAG GUY That's the whole thing about passion. Passion is great. You can have passion and you can be enthusiastic about what you want to do and you want to change the world and all that stuff.

But if you're not committed to it, it doesn't mean anything.

And most importantly, you have to be committed to it and have an observable, visual action where someone can say, 'Dude. That guy is committed.'

TATTOO ARTIST There's this club you join when you get an area of your body tattooed that can't be covered up by clothes. It's called the 'all done club.' It's what you do when you decide you're completely committed.

As far as having a passion for this job, and why I've always done this job, it got to the point where I tattooed my hands and my knuckles. I got my knuckles tattooed maybe ten years ago with the words Fate and Hope.

When you don't have your hands or your neck tattooed, then I could put on a suit and tie and be ready to go. But when I tattooed my hands and my knuckles, that was part of my self conscious saying 'this is it.' Because it's what you're supposed to do when you're all done. Because it does lock you in.

I could be a banker in 5 years. Obviously, not anymore. Because this is what I want to do. Mentally, that commitment is worth it. It provides clarity. You just have to figure out what you want and commit to doing it. I knew I wanted to do this, so I committed.

BOXING GYM OWNER You can't psyche yourself out. Because then you hesitate and you just get nailed. It's committing. If you're going to get in the ring, just commit and throw punches.

Risk

CELEBRITY CHEF It was my third and final day at the restaurant. I had such a great day that third day. They were like, 'Okay, tomorrow, we're going to show you how to pick arugula and clean a rack of veal.' I couldn't bear to say, 'Well actually this is my last day if you remember I was only supposed to be here three days, and I have a flight home tomorrow.' I couldn't bear to say it. It just wouldn't come out of my mouth. I was just like, 'Okay, cool. A rack of veal tomorrow? Great!' I left the restaurant and I was like, 'I have to learn how to cut that veal. I can't go home. I've got a veal to cut!'

So I went back the next day. I missed my plane. I called my boyfriend at the time and said 'I love you. But I just can't come home right now. I just can't do it. I'm sorry.' I went back to the restaurant again, and again, and again, and again and I just couldn't leave. I wound up staying at that restaurant for four and a half years.

ENGINEERING ENTREPRENEUR Starting a company is like blackjack. You don't have to win every hand, but you have to have enough chips to continue playing the game, and you have to win back some of those chips every once in a while too.

REAL ESTATE DEVELOPER People have told me that I must like to gamble because I'm in this business. I don't like to gamble at all. I'm not a guy that goes to Las Vegas or does anything gambling.

It's not gambling at all. **It's a calculated risk in development.**

HOTEL OWNER You have to take emotion out of your business decisions. The sooner you take emotion out of your business decisions, the better you are. I've booked some bands that I liked, and guess what? They didn't do well. So I try to use facts to book the bands. I look at box office results across the country.

Emotion, whether it's managing people, disciplinary action, booking talent, even in your private life. The more your decision is based on fact, the better off you are.

MUSIC PRODUCER

A lot of spreadsheets have led me to where I am today.

Risk

REPORTER You have to be able to move to Medford, Oregon and to Jackson, Mississippi and spend those years out in the middle of nowhere. It's rough. We left our families and friends and whoever else behind to move to the middle of nowhere to do this. So you really have to like it a lot.

DOCUMENTARIAN Maybe it was kind of crazy. I don't know. So I went over to Iraq to help Iraqis talk to the world. It was kind of like, a little bit insane to go over with the attitude like, 'I'm going to go to Iraq and we'll see what happens.'

BASKETBALL COACH It was kind of a crazy thing when I took this job at Arizona. I went from a team that was seeded number 4 in the country to a team that was last out of ten teams in the Pac 10. And I had a lifetime contract at Iowa. In Arizona, they only gave you one year by state law. So it was taking a big risk.

BROWNIE PRODUCER The parents definitely thought I was a little bit nuts. I had a corporate job at Proctor & Gamble. I had a good college education from Stanford. My business partner was the top sales person for the local Spanish television station. So yeah, when we told our parents that we were going to give up that and go start a brownie business, they were very skeptical and very concerned.

when you choose this road.

Yellowstone Park, WY

CELEBRITY CHEF There were a lot of moments in work where I was like, 'Am I crazy?' And there's no one to ask. Other than your parents, who are crazy anyway.

CO-WORKING ATTENDANT It's all embodied in this concept of embracing chaos. Everyday something crazy is going to happen. There's nothing I can do about it. How can I capture that energy and spin it some place positive? It's one day at a time. What's next? Tomorrow is next. That's as far as I know.

SOFTWARE EXECUTIVE There is always a sense of adventure and the unknown. I definitely like that. I thrive on that. If you're someone who doesn't like the unknown, go work for another company. Don't be an entrepreneur.

HUMANITARIAN I don't always think about the fact that I'm a pioneer until after the fact. I think less about myself and more about my goals and what I'm trying to accomplish. I think if I thought too much about myself in these roles I'd probably get pretty nervous and have a lot of questions and doubts. But I try to focus on what I hope to accomplish. When you think about things bigger than oneself, I think you keep your focus on your mission and on your passion.

STARTUPOLOGIST

The hallmark of entrepreneurship is dealing with the little failures to get to the ultimate big win.

CROSSWORD PUZZLE CREATOR Failure is a hot stove. Once you touch it, you never forget how it felt or where it is. So you always walk around it. And you really just want to avoid that experience once more. True entrepreneurs see 'getting burned' as the true, early level course. It's Entrepreneurship 101- 'Getting burned.'

ENTREPRENEURSHIP EXPERT Failure is just another outcome. I think that if we wouldn't treat it with as much severity as a 'failure,' versus 'this was a success,' we just look at it as another outcome. And then go on to the following outcome and the next outcome. I think we have too much attached to failure.

So what if you 'fail?' American society, fortunately, is very forgiving. They do give second chances. And third chances and fourth chances.

Please Excuse Our Mess, As We Clean Up From Storm Damage.

HARRISON COUNTY SAND BEACH DEPT.

Biloxi, MS

THAT GUY How did I get here today? Well, it's all failure. Pretty much my whole life has been a failure. You usually only see the happy parts. No one ever sees failure.

I got an internship with Microsoft my junior year at UC Berkeley. Normally, anyone who gets an internship gets the job. **I was rejected.** I had a job offer at Google pre-IPO and they rescinded it for some reason. I don't know, maybe they didn't like me. I would have been really rich, pre-IPO Google.

I dropped a resume at Facebook because I like the web and I like people. I did a lot of college marketing to college businesses and so they offered me a job. I went in there, did product management for seven months. I made a lot of features, met a lot of people. Worked nonstop. It was a lot of fun. And then, I wasn't good there? **I'm not sure what happened there, but I did get laid off.** Marky and I maybe didn't get along, I'm not sure.

Things happen. I have a tough time getting over things. But you just have to keep moving forward. When you move on to the next thing you kind of put things in the past. You have to accept it. What I've done with the Facebook thing is being honest with myself. So I got laid off. That's a really hard thing for people. Especially at a company where I'd be a millionaire.

So it's on to the next thing and becoming a millionaire in other

ways. As many things that have gone wrong, in terms of getting fired or the jobs I didn't get hired, I'm satisfied with what I've accomplished. I'm proud of it.

CEO The reality of the matter is if you take a risk and it doesn't work out, it's okay. What you'll realize is that in the number of initiatives and risk taking that you take, you'll always have a disappointment.

The best possible way to overcome that is to move on. Is to admit it, and then move on. Because people will remember the good and lasting things.

GARDENER I say the only thing that makes me an expert is that I've killed more plants than you have.

CASINO PRESIDENT One of the things I've noticed when I talk to people who start their own businesses is they see where they are and where they want to be. They don't see all the bull that's in the middle. They just plow right through that.

When I was offered President at Prim, I didn't have any operational experience at all. I'd never held a position in operations. So for a little bit I'm thinking, 'Okay. What do I know about running the property? It's not where I've spent my time and my focus.'

It dawned on me. 'I'm smart. I can figure this out. I know I can. Why would I say no? Why wouldn't I at least go for it?'

The advice I would give is to get rid of your limiting beliefs.

Get real clear on what you want. Get real clear on what looks like fun to you at that moment in your life. And don't listen to all the chatter on why you can't have it. Because it's those limited beliefs that will paralyze you from acting on opportunities.

New York, NY

BANJO PLAYER When you're not afraid, and you're just chasing after something and you don't know any better, you're just unstoppable.

ORAL HISTORIAN It may scare you. It scares me. I think, 'I love writing about this, but who the hell is going to buy this?'

Although I usually find that if you really get inside yourself and put it out there, that's what everyone else thinks too. We're all the same. We all relate.

SCREENWRITER *History of Violence* was a very personal script for me. I had gotten the job by being brought in to pitch, and was told by the executive, 'We really just want to get to know you. **You're not going to get the job.** We're talking to four or five really big writers, but I want you to come in and if you're impressive we can get you back in for something else.'

I took that as a license to pitch the story that I wanted to tell. I pitched the story I wanted, and they ended up going with me instead of these big writers. That's a very valuable lesson.

SERIAL ENTREPRENEUR If it's a good idea, by the nature of a good idea, you will get a lot of negative feedback. A good idea will receive more negative feedback than a lot of bad ideas because it will have a contrarian hypothesis.

Really groundbreaking, good ideas have a contrarian nature. They contradict the common wisdom. They contradict common sense. A little bit, not completely, but there is an element of that.

That's why no one else is doing it. Because no one else thinks it's feasible.

Rancho Cucamonga, CA

CAREER COACH People have a million reasons why they can't do whatever it is. And that's fine. Because you can do whatever you want. And you can not do whatever you want. The scary part is when you say to someone, 'This is what I'm going to do.'

MUSCULAR DYSTROPHY ADVOCATE I think the key is just changing the mindset. We actually have a word we use. It's on the back of my wheelchair. The word is 'Handicrap.'

It's a fun word to throw out there. A lot of people with disabilities have their own personal handicrap. It might be hiding behind their disability. They might put up roadblocks by saying, 'Hey, I can't do that. I've got these chair challenges.' Whether you have a disability or not, that 'handicrap' mindset takes away your excuse and forces you to plan and prepare.

I actually once heard someone say, What's the worst that can happen? They can't eat you.' There's something really to that. You know? They can't eat you.

POUND CAKE PRODUCER Nothing is impossible. So much is how you think about things. If you think in terms of 'I can't do it,' all that will come up in your mind are the things that you can't do. If you think of what you can do, possibilities will show up. Everything that you focus on has that impact.

PR FIRM PARTNER Don't wait until you're 60 years old and look back to say 'What if.' The worst thing is to go through life and have regrets. It's a matter of doing it and being willing to fail. Be willing to learn and pick yourself up again.

THAT GUY The advice would be to maybe consider doing whatever it is that I'm scared of doing. Not make stupid decisions, but maybe be a little more risk preferential. Be willing to take more risks. But that's the thing! **Why am I not taking more risks today then?**

PLAYBOY PLAYMATE Hey, you're only young and good looking for so long.

What are you risking?

Glendale, AZ

RAPPER

It takes confidence. There has to be some talent involved too... and hustle. You put all those things together and it equates to... sometimes a success, sometimes a starving artist.

RAPPER

My main thing was I wanted to build self sufficiency. I'm not trying to use my time and my hours towards building up somebody else's dream. I wasn't always making a good living, but I was not trying to have another job when I could do something else.

Roll the Credits: *P210*

Hard Work

'Hard work' should be a no brainer right?

We've all heard sayings like 'there's no shortcut to success' and 'you get out what you put in.' But there is a real distinction between what our interviewees considered hard work and what people who dislike their jobs consider hard work.

As glamorous as Pursue the Passion may sound, it required a lot of hard work. When we first were getting started, Jay and I had to build a website, book interviews, find places to stay, and raise thousands of dollars to get the wheels on our tour turning. We went to work every morning at 8am, sharing a desk in my apartment, and wouldn't leave until physical exhaustion set in. We did that for months until all of those sponsorship proposals, interview requests, and promotion tactics started to produce results.

We worked harder than we ever had in our lives. Jay, a college graduate, was getting $6/hour. I was losing $6/hour. We obviously weren't working for the money. We ate frozen food for 30 days and worked an unhealthy amount of hours because we cared about creating something cool for ourselves and for the future beneficiaries of Pursue the Passion.

Do you think we would have put in the same kind of effort for a job we didn't care about?

When you don't enjoy your job all the work is hard. You're constantly watching the clock and largely judge your 'hard work' on the amount of time that you're working. People who are passionate about what they do make work a large part of their life by choice. There's a distortion of time when you are doing something you love. For the people we interviewed, 'hard work' was not a quantitative declaration, but a qualitative statement. The passion they have for their career brings the hard work out, rather than having the career call for hard work to be put in.

Hard work is the element in which people spend the longest amount of time while pursing a passion. It's the most fundamental of the three things, and the one we have the most control over.

NO CRUISING

THREE TIMES PAST SAME
POINT WITHIN FOUR HOURS
IS CRUISING

C.V.C.SECT. 21100(K) L.B.M.C. CHAP. 10.66
CITY OF LONG BEACH

Long Beach, CA

ZOO DIRECTOR I'd say the most transferable skill that's got me the furthest is how to use a rake and a shovel.

PHYSICIST In every experiment, it's 99% sweat and 1% ingenuity.

BEER BREWER How do you get a job as a beer reviewer? You have to drink longer and more than anyone else.

VIDEO GAME DESIGNER The majority of the time you're working your tail off. There have been a couple times where I slept in my cube.

SERIAL ENTREPRENEUR At this time last year, we had four employees that were unpaid. We didn't get much sleep. We pulled all nighters twice a week last year. It was a really challenging time.

VOICEOVER AGENT Our first year here I worked almost every weekend, Saturday and Sunday to keep this place afloat.

TATTOO ARTIST It was hard starting out. I had to go through many, many steps.

SCREENWRITER The hardest part is conjuring something up from nothing.

REGISTERED NURSE It's not all glamour. Sometimes you have to change a diaper on an eighty year old person.

PIZZA SHOP OWNER The restaurant business doesn't stop at 5. You can't take Fridays, Saturdays, and Sundays off. You can't take Monday, Tuesday, Wednesday off. You have to be in it for 80 to 100 hours a week. But if you're doing a job right, it's not a job. It's just social. About 100 social hours a week.

EXECUTIVE CHEF It's not a pretty world out there. When you start out you're at the lowest of the lowest of low life forms. You're in charge of the dishwashing area. It's more of learning intestinal fortitude and self discipline than learning how to be a chef.

SOFTWARE ENGINEER I don't really know how to state this, but people here work really, really hard. They work long hours. People will work with their heads down for sixty hours a week, eighty hours a week, maybe more. I've been there. When it comes time to take a break, you take 2 or 3 days and relax. After you ship a product, a lot of people take exotic vacations.

REAL ESTATE INVESTOR That job at Dominic's was tough. These were sixty, seventy hour weeks I was working. Some people would say, 'It's just not worth it to go through that.' When I was at Dominic's the stress was so much that I had purple spots on my forearms from the stress. I had a condition called Lichen Planus. It doesn't hurt you. It's not painful. It's just related to stress.

Because I was working Saturdays and Sundays. I was drinking a lot of coffee. But, I loved my job. I loved what I was doing because I knew that I was having a big impact on this company. So I didn't mind working the 60, 70 hour weeks.

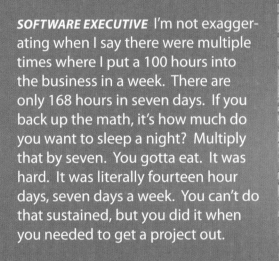

SOFTWARE EXECUTIVE I'm not exaggerating when I say there were multiple times where I put a 100 hours into the business in a week. There are only 168 hours in seven days. If you back up the math, it's how much do you want to sleep a night? Multiply that by seven. You gotta eat. It was hard. It was literally fourteen hour days, seven days a week. You can't do that sustained, but you did it when you needed to get a project out.

ENTREPRENEURSHIP EXPERT People are looking for the key to success. People are hungry for that information. But they're not willing to work on it. It's sad.

The biggest best seller this year was *The Secret*. Just by its very name, people want to know 'What's the secret?' And the fact is that there is no secret. We don't want to accept that, because most of us want to find a shortcut. Most of us would rather win the lottery than work hard. We want to be able to cheat our way. We want to find the magic so we don't have to go through all those other steps, and really be forced to deal with all the unexpected things with good luck and bad luck.

But I think we gotta give that up. The sooner we give that up, the sooner we can start to work for and earn our success.

MOTIVATIONAL SPEAKER My mom did not want me to learn sign language. In fact, she put me in a public school rather than a deaf school. It was not easy because I was surrounded by people who could hear. I was often left out. I had to learn how to adapt. But it worked well for me because I'm able to function in the larger world. 99% of the world can hear. My mom wanted me to be able to do that.

It took me probably twenty years to learn how to speak. How my mother would do it is she would have a booklet with pictures and words underneath them. We would go through the booklet and she would point to the picture, and then point to the word. She would have me put my hand on her throat and she would say the word. I'd feel it. She'd put my hand back on my throat and I would repeat after her. I would continue to do it until I got it right. We did that forever.

Adversity does not discriminate. No one is immune from adversity. Some just have more than others. I've had it. You've had it. I have come to see adversity as opportunity to grow and learn. An opportunity to get smarter. An opportunity to see things in a different way. Instead of thinking, 'Why me?'

I used to do that. Believe me, I used to think, 'Why me? I'm deaf. I don't want to be deaf. Why? Why! Why!' I used to think that. But now I'm like, 'Why not?' I now know that I have a special purpose. All it takes is a lot of perseverance. Adversity is our teacher. We learn things through adversity.

Sedona, AZ

DOCUMENTARIAN If you want it, it will happen. It's not going to be easy. I'm not going to sit here and tell you that you can do anything you want. But I really think that determination gets you a lot. Simply being willing and being brave and maybe getting free credit cards like I did.

DRUG MANUFACTURER I think of life as a flight of stairs. Being a science geek too, in physical chemistry there is phase change. You're inputting a bunch of energy into water and nothing changes, nothing changes, then all of a sudden, BAM! It changes phases. That's like a stair step.

Humans in general as we grow we get some kind of challenge. We struggle and work hard on it and then all of a sudden one day it clicks. You feel like you jumped up to that next level and you feel happy.

Then you start cruising and you don't think about it so much, then all of a sudden you hit some other thing that causes you to think hard and force change.

BAM! You're up another stair.

From my experience, you need a little strife or some adversity in order for you to realize that.

New Orleans, LA

Always follow your dreams!!! I love you... Mom xoxoxo

CELEBRITY CHEF

It was a particularly unnerving day. As the day progressed, I just got more and more rattled.

I'm broke. I'm hungry. I'm tired, grouchy and overworked. I started to get

a desire to return home and eat a bagel and watch fourteen episodes of the Brady Bunch.

The sous chef came in and he's like, "You've been here six months and we haven't been paying you, have we?" And I'm like, "Nooooo, you have not." He said, "Okay, I'll see what I can do."

Guy Savoy called me down to his office. On the way to his office I was thinking that I would either get paid or asked to leave. I wasn't sure. At the time I was making a big bowl of potatoes with butter and was mixing it. So I had just a sheet of butter on my hands and elbows. I'm in his office and the butter is landing on the floor and going, 'Drip...Drip...Drip.'

Guy Savoy looks at me and he's like, "Here's some money. You're doing a great job. Keep up the good work."

That was one of, and is still, other than the birth of my daughter, one of the most gratifying moments of my life.

I realized I could slog through all this and make money. I won't be rich. But I can make money and I can sustain my-self and do what I really love. It made everything worth it.

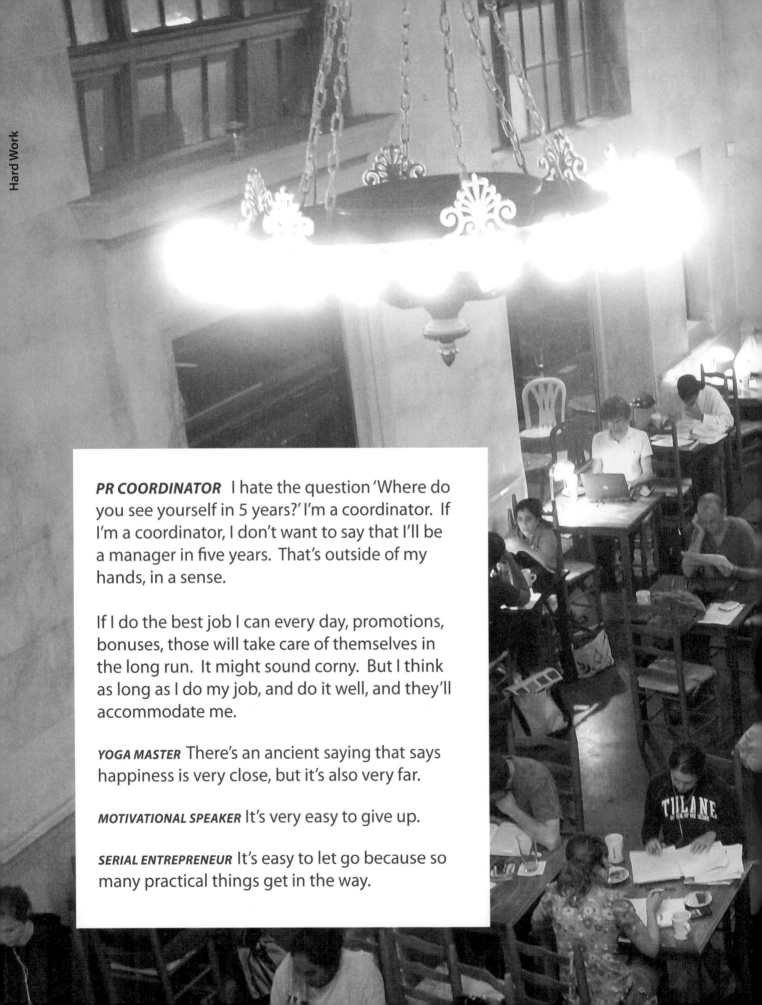

PR COORDINATOR I hate the question 'Where do you see yourself in 5 years?' I'm a coordinator. If I'm a coordinator, I don't want to say that I'll be a manager in five years. That's outside of my hands, in a sense.

If I do the best job I can every day, promotions, bonuses, those will take care of themselves in the long run. It might sound corny. But I think as long as I do my job, and do it well, and they'll accommodate me.

YOGA MASTER There's an ancient saying that says happiness is very close, but it's also very far.

MOTIVATIONAL SPEAKER It's very easy to give up.

SERIAL ENTREPRENEUR It's easy to let go because so many practical things get in the way.

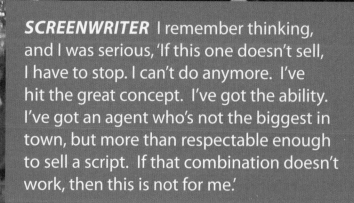

MOTIVATIONAL SPEAKER But I keep telling myself that if I give up, what then? I'll never know what I could have done. I have that on my mind. If I give up, what could happen when I get older? I'll be thinking that I could have done this. I don't want that on my conscience.

SCREENWRITER I remember thinking, and I was serious, 'If this one doesn't sell, I have to stop. I can't do anymore. I've hit the great concept. I've got the ability. I've got an agent who's not the biggest in town, but more than respectable enough to sell a script. If that combination doesn't work, then this is not for me.'

It reminds me of those idiots who are broke on their ass and they're saying 'Well, this script, I'm going to sell this script!' I literally got to that point. I was down to less than $200 in the bank. And then, Paramount bought my script. For life altering sums of money.

After years of struggling, it was so strange, because all of a sudden the game plan was to sell a big commercial script and then start writing movies that really matter to you. It took forever to get in the door, but once I got in the door, it was doing what I wanted to do.

New Orleans, LA

83

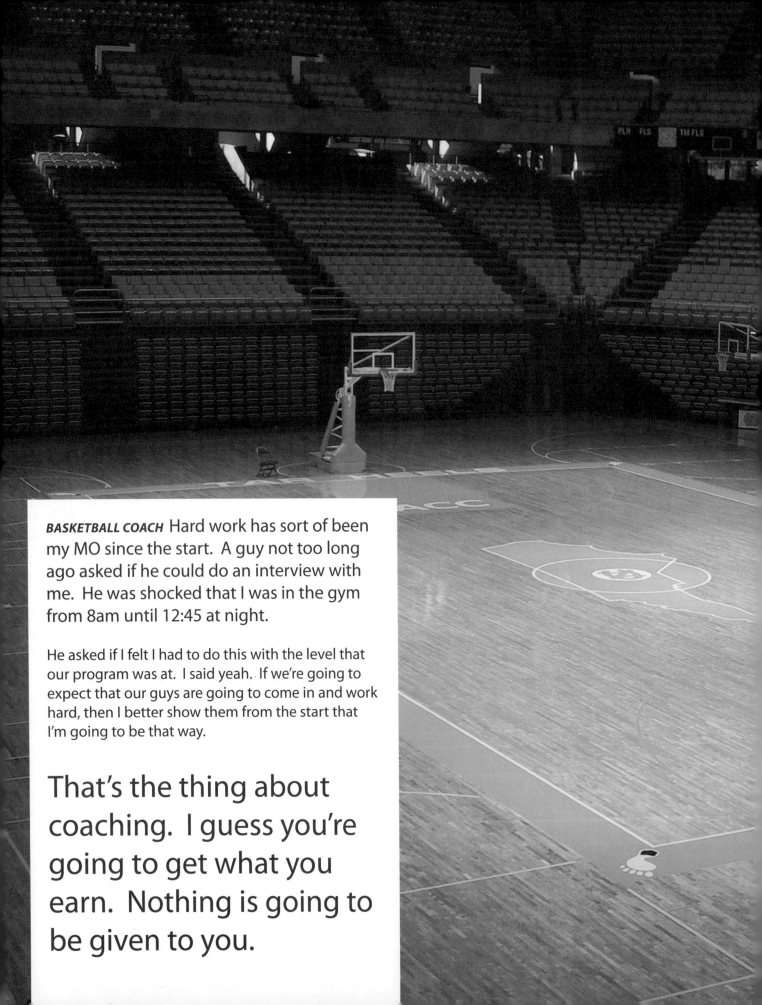

BASKETBALL COACH Hard work has sort of been my MO since the start. A guy not too long ago asked if he could do an interview with me. He was shocked that I was in the gym from 8am until 12:45 at night.

He asked if I felt I had to do this with the level that our program was at. I said yeah. If we're going to expect that our guys are going to come in and work hard, then I better show them from the start that I'm going to be that way.

That's the thing about coaching. I guess you're going to get what you earn. Nothing is going to be given to you.

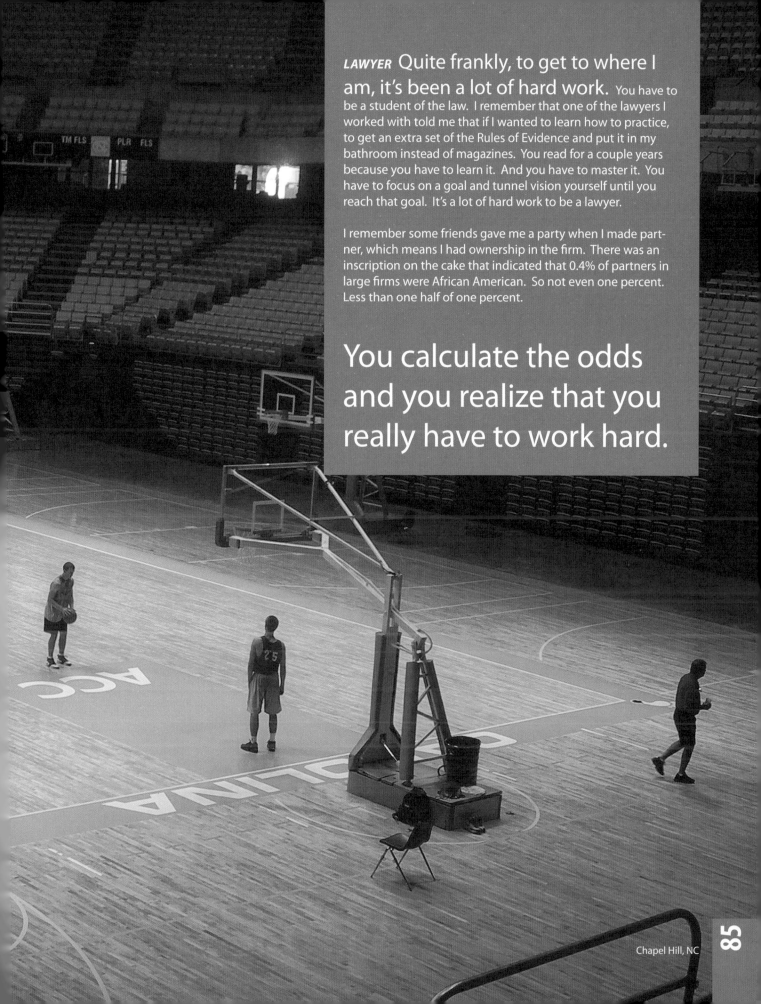

LAWYER Quite frankly, to get to where I am, it's been a lot of hard work. You have to be a student of the law. I remember that one of the lawyers I worked with told me that if I wanted to learn how to practice, to get an extra set of the Rules of Evidence and put it in my bathroom instead of magazines. You read for a couple years because you have to learn it. And you have to master it. You have to focus on a goal and tunnel vision yourself until you reach that goal. It's a lot of hard work to be a lawyer.

I remember some friends gave me a party when I made partner, which means I had ownership in the firm. There was an inscription on the cake that indicated that 0.4% of partners in large firms were African American. So not even one percent. Less than one half of one percent.

You calculate the odds and you realize that you really have to work hard.

Chapel Hill, NC

MARKETING CONSULTANT I keep hearing about all these overnight successes. **The average overnight success takes seventeen years.** The media notices them when they become a phenomenon.

Where have they been for seventeen years?

They've been behind the scenes training. Making the distinctions. Being disciplined. Focusing on their passion. You look at most of the athletes. They have an average of seventeen to twenty-one years of total dedication to the sport.

The same thing with business people. With CEO's. With product designers. They've been paying their dues and paying their dues and paying their dues. And then, they have the breakthrough.

San Francisco, CA

BASKETBALL COACH When I got to Division I it was seventeen years of background of coaching. Thirteen years at the high school level and four years at Long Beach City College. In my eighteenth year I became the head coach of Long Beach State.

FOOTWEAR DESIGNER It took me twelve years to get here.

BEER BREWER I was a beer merchant. I started selling beer in 1978. Which makes me the person that's been selling crab beer longer than anyone else.

HEALTHCARE ENTREPRENEUR Finally, we're fulfilling some things that we saw back in 1990 that we really wanted to do. I love seeing ideas that we've had for a decade finally come to fruition in a very rational environment.

GARDENER My garden took ten years of prep work because of the berry vines. Here's how bad it was. By the time my dad and I made it all the way back in the corner of my backyard, we found a baby blue VW Bug. We fixed it up and sold it for $750. It was sweet. That paid for a CAT to scrape the land.

Chicago, IL

REPORTER I had that sense of wanting everything now when I graduated. But it went away fast when I started carrying a forty pound tripod through the snow.

BROWNIE PRODUCER When I was young, I had visions of retiring by age 40. Looking back, that was a little unrealistic.

When we quit our corporate jobs, we didn't have any wage. And that was for three years. We were full time brownies, no salary for three years. Just living off of savings and family support. And brownies.

Then it took five years for us to be able to pay ourselves back with the same salary we left in the corporate job. It was eight years before the company had a positive net worth. And then it got a little easier and easier after that.

PR FIRM OWNER I think too many people aren't willing to accept that it takes a long time to be successful. They aspire to be entrepreneurs but they're not willing to go through that pain period of either going without a significant salary for x number of months or longer, or something goes wrong and the business doesn't pan out. And they say, 'Well, I tried.'

CELEBRITY CHEF I had a woman in here the other week who was 24. She said to me, 'By the time I'm 30 I want to have my own restaurant. I want to be married. I want to have two kids. By the time I'm 30. I have 6 years. No problem.'

I'm just looking at her like, I know I talked like you when I was your age. And I turned around and I'm 38, and I have half of that. I opened up my mouth and I started to say something, and then I just said screw it. She'll figure it out.

NAME TAG GUY I was interviewing on the *Today Show* and waiting in the green room. There's this other guy there. He was an older guy, a well known expert on bugs and ticks for dogs. He said, 'Congratulations. Your book is great. You're going to have a really great career.

In about 5 years, you're going to start making money and it's going to be great.'

I was like, 'Really? *Is that how long it takes?*'

ANIMATOR My advice would be to learn to eat Top Ramen.

VIDEO GAME DESIGNER The biggest thing about getting into video games is that you have to be patient. You're not making a lot of money right off the bat. I mean, I lived with six dudes in an apartment for the first year and a half because I was making like, seven bucks an hour straight out of college. I had more money when I was in college than my first couple years in games. You have to be willing to be patient and make no money in the beginning.

BASKETBALL COACH Sean Elliot stayed here all four years. He had a chance to come out after his junior year, and his mother basically said that he was going to finish this. The contracts he could have gotten after his junior year were $6 million less than the contract he got after four years here. It really paid off for him.

PHYSICAL THERAPIST It isn't easy. You have to dedicate yourself.

CIRCUS LADY Dedicate yourself and focus. Life is all about juggling your responsibilities and balancing your priorities. You know how you keep balance, and this is true on the wire, is that you don't stay in one place and balance. You keep taking the next step forward. If you can't concentrate for 'x' amount of time, you're not going to be able to walk the tightrope.

I-90, Washington

CELEBRITY CHEF I think a lot of people have the attitude of, 'Well, I'll just work here. Until I figure out how I'm going to buy a loom and play the harp.' You have to go to the harp player's house and ask how to play a harp. You have to, like, bleed until you figure it out. That's what you have to do.

AUTHOR One of the things about careers is that sometimes you have to do things you don't want to do to get to where you want to go.

NAME TAG GUY How many speeches have I done? I don't know. Are we counting the times when I was in the middle of nowhere at 7am talking to a Bible study group of seven old men who didn't care about me? Does that count?

Venice, CA

New York, NY

Seattle, WA

Chicago, IL

Seattle, WA

West Yellowstone, WY

VENTURE CAPITALIST I think really, really good entrepreneurs just keep going and going.

HUMANITARIAN They call me the Energizer Bunny around here. I keep long hours and keep a very demanding pace. But again, it's because I feel very committed to things I'm working on with a lot of passion.

HEALTHCARE ENTREPRENEUR I think people can be very happy without having that extra boost of passion in what they're doing. They can just enjoy it enough to get through their day, put in their hours, and still have a good time without watching the clock. But, it's not that thrill that you get when you truly passionate about doing something new.

VENTURE CAPITALIST You can't work fifty, sixty, eighty hours a week if you don't care about the thing you're trying to create.

FIRE CAPTAIN The process to become a firefighter is extremely competitive. Thousands of people are applying and participating in a process where only dozens of jobs are available. It took me four years to get through the process. It can be discouraging.

The difference between the people that stick with the process and those who don't is you separate the one who really have a passion for it. There are some of those that are looking at the job for other reasons. Those other reasons could be that they just need a job, or they're enamored with the prestige of the job.

ART DIRECTOR Prestige is not enough.

FIRE CAPTAIN The ones that really have that deep down desire to help people on a really intimate level, those people stay with the process.

Phoenix, AZ

GUITAR SCHOOL INSTRUCTOR When I first started teaching guitar lessons, I was hustling up and down the streets of New York City. I was putting flyers on lamp posts. I put flyers up all over the place. I was literally running from block to block so I could be faster.

I was on the corner of 86th and York Avenue, and I saw this homeless guy with a shopping cart full of bottles and cans. He was running the other direction from garbage can to garbage can, pulling out cans and bottles. He wanted to get them before anyone else got them.

I look to the left and see this limousine drive past. In the back, there's this guy talking on the telephone. And I could tell he was working.

New York, NY

I thought, 'Wait a minute. That homeless guy is going all out and he's making $4 an hour. I'm going all out and I'm making $15 an hour. And that guy is going all out and maybe he's making thousands of dollars an hour.'

So I thought, 'If I'm going to go all out, why don't I go all out in a way that really works for me?'

DOCUMENTARIAN I mean, I had the 9-5 job. I was working it. It was the kind of thing where I would be there at the end of the day, and I was empty inside.

I was sitting at a desk for eight hours and not enjoying the work. Now I sit at a desk for twelve hours and love the work. How crazy is that?

-0231 KEEP OUR BEACHES

SUMMER MOVIES SUNDAY NIGHTS @ 8PM THROUGH LABOR DAY

RULES

The Endless Summer

on
KDOC-TV

DOC-TV
CLASSICS

www.kdoc.tv

KEARU
101 FM

REATEST HITS ON EARTH

San Clemente, CA

SERIAL ENTREPRENEUR Life is so much richer when you're doing something you care about. It's not comparable at all.

There's no comparison to a life where you're going to work, doing something you don't really enjoy, for forty hours a week. Compared to going to work and doing exactly what you want to do forty hours a week. It's like light and dark.

When you're doing something you love, time expands. Time goes away. Weekends go away. Yeah you work all the time, but it's not the same. Time feels infinite. You lose yourself in a lot of moments.

When I graduated from college I took a job that I wasn't really excited about. I worked there for four years. Eight hours every day. My mentality was like, 'Oh good, its lunch! Thank God. Oh good, its dinner! Thank God. I don't want to go to bed tonight because then I have to wake up and go back tomorrow.'

That seemed like an eternity.

But I don't think like that anymore. The whole meaning of time has changed for me.

MARKETING CONSULTANT

Is there a formula for success?

Well, it's interesting. One of the things we talk about is distinctions. The definition of distinction is the difference that makes the difference. What's the difference between a glass of orange juice and a screwdriver? Vodka. It's the difference that makes the difference.

If you think about what an expert is, an expert is someone who merely makes higher levels of distinctions. So when you look at a great filmmaker, why, film after film, does Spielberg get it?

Because, he has the ability to make these distinctions. Lighting. Actors. Set. Background. He can make those levels of distinction and understand how they impact the emotion of the film.

AUDIBLE FIRE

UL
®

LISTED
11Z4

25 mA

120V AC

TO REMO
BOLT

Phoenix, AZ

What being successful is about, is getting into a field where you're passionate enough to keep studying long enough to make those levels of distinctions. Because if you get in a field that you're not that passionate about, five o'clock comes and you want to do anything besides what you've been doing.

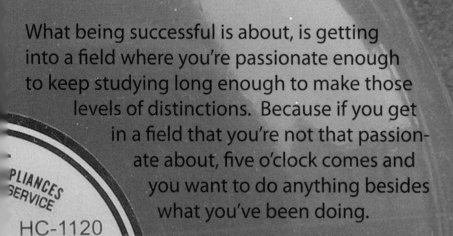

When I'm passionate about work, when five o'clock comes, what do you want to do? You want to stay there. You want to keep learning. You want to study with the masters. You want to be immersed in this, deeper. You keep chasing it. When you love what you do so much there's no distinction between work and play.

That's why finding your passion is so critical. When you get there, and you stay there, and you're focused there, you have the breakthrough.

Hard Work

RESTAURANT MANAGER When I cook with the cooks in the kitchen, you have to really put your heart on the plate. You have to give it more than just the technical. You could sear that thing perfectly and put it just the way it was meant to be, but it takes more to it. Because if you don't let your heart out of you, you'll never have an exceptional product. You'll have a great product, but you'll never have an exceptional product.

We try to make sure that it's a passion. Food is luscious and sexy. Cooking is like making love. You can slap it down, throw it in the fire and forget about it.

Or you can caress it and make sure you're all over it and you are making sure you're focused on it.

OUTDOOR ADVERTISER To get to the breakthrough…I don't know how to put it. Maybe you call it an accidental happening. But really, it isn't an accidental happening. It's years of hard work! And experience and being able to pull it off.

GOLF INSTRUCTOR I come to *play* golf. I don't come to *work* golf.

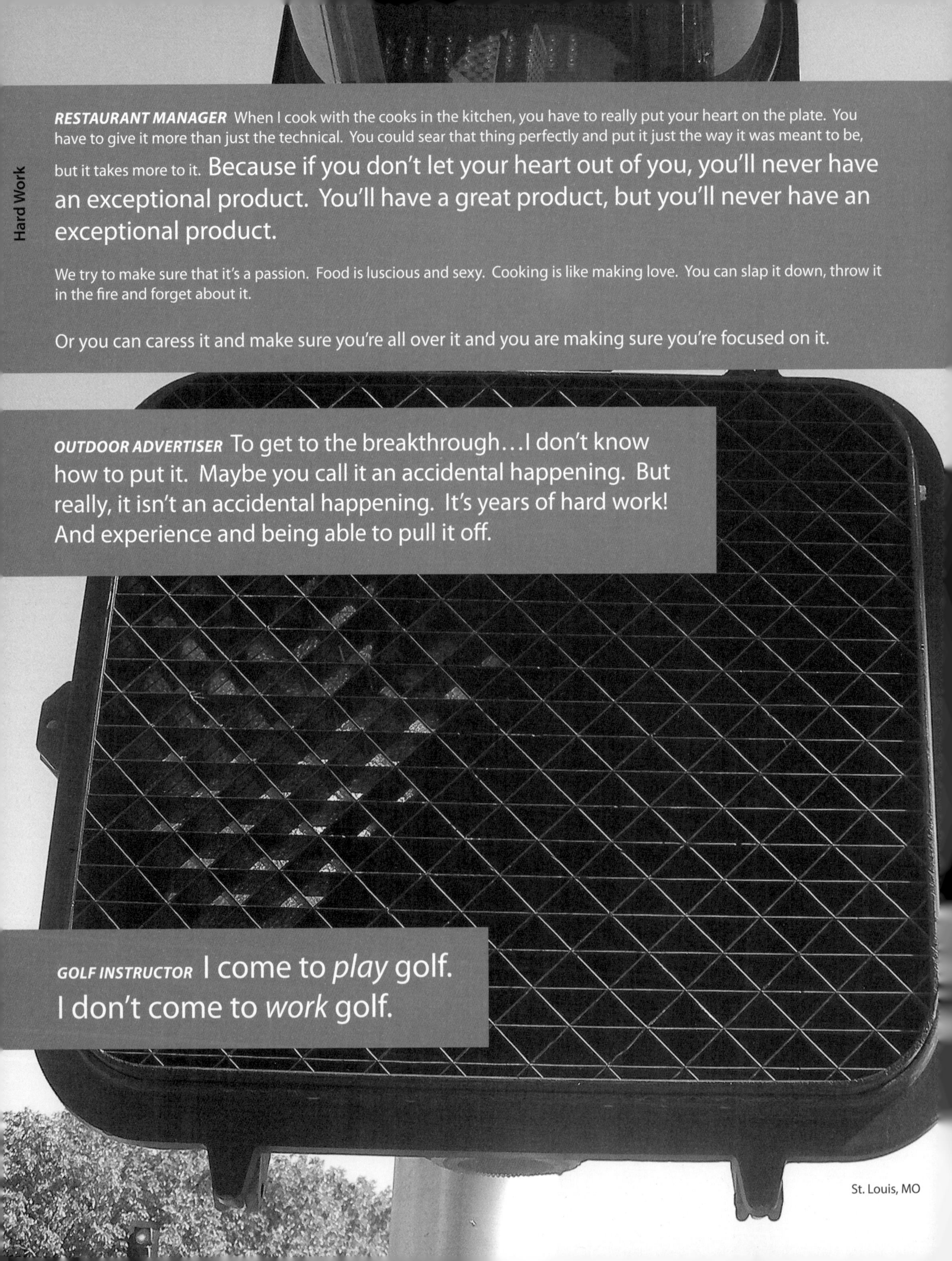

St. Louis, MO

BASEBALL STATISTICIAN In terms in flat out advice, there's no one route in, but you gotta work your butt off to get in. I feel like I was knocking on this enormous door for two, three years. If you count back the years when I didn't even know this was an opportunity, you might say it was five to ten years.

I was just pounding, bloody knuckles and all, waiting for the doors to open. Once they opened, it was like, 'Hey! Where've you been?'

SERIAL ENTREPRENEUR These things happen unpredictably. The best things in life you can't really predict or calculate or plan. They sort of happen to you. They feel external. There's an element of serendipity around the best things.

COMMUNICATIONS DIRECTOR The best definition of luck is when hard work meets opportunity. I think that's why a lot of people find themselves where they are. It's the law of unintended consequences. Sometimes it just happens.

BASKETBALL COACH You think you're going to be good, but you know that there are going to be other teams that are going to be good also. You set that standard immediately that you're going to reach for the very best. You practice for perfection, knowing that you're never going to achieve perfection. But that doesn't mean you stop striving for it.

ENTREPRENEURSHIP EXPERT Sometimes, only inertia keeps you going. But if you have a vision, and if you can find an economic way to keep going, there's an opportunity for success.

ANIMATOR The point is that if you want to do it bad enough, no one can talk you out of it. But it takes a lot of work and you have to keep at it and not get frustrated. You're going to get rejected constantly. That's really hard. Artists are sensitive. We take red lights personally. You just have to be persistent and not give up. Keep plugging away.

BANJO PLAYER It's like what golfers say.
One great shot is what keeps you coming back.

Lusk, WY

It's not that it's there all the time, it's that the ability for it to happen is always right there.

Part II: The Passion

Nashville, TN

When we got back from our tour we decided that we wanted to keep Pursue the Passion going. We had gathered too much valuable information and met too many people in need of that information to not share it. We went back to Jobing.com with a plan and they agreed to continue Pursue the Passion as a program of the Jobing Foundation.

We created an educational program for students to do their own interviews, grew the website into a resourceful tool for classes to use, and were asked to speak about our experiences by conference organizers, schools, and companies.

The topic of these speeches? Passion.

These speeches about passion brought on a whole series of new questions for us. What is passion? Where does it come from? How do you find it? How do you sustain it? How can you encourage it? We started to look back on our interviews to find the answer.

HOME   ABOUT PTP   CAREER INTERVIEWS   JOURNEY BLOG   CONTACT

"Millions of people are looking at something I produced."

Various Entrepreneurs
Location: Phoenix, Arizona

Watch the Video & Read the Interview

Los Angeles, CA

Jobing Foundation

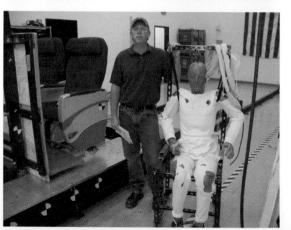

SERIAL ENTREPRENEUR

We definitely felt like doing this idea was worth it as a non successful idea. Even if it was mildly successful it was still worth it. Even if no one else knew about it, and it was just us, we would have done it. And that's the difference.

SERIAL ENTREPRENEUR
I tried to start maybe ten companies. I have a list of just wacky ideas. I tried to start a DVD vending machine company. I tried to start an online clothing rental company. I also tried to start a robot company where the robots were connected to the internet and would perform episodes together. It's not that those ideas failed, but it's like a couple months later I was wondering why I was doing it.

*Roll the Credits: **P209***

Significance

Why do people work the jobs they work?

There are thousands of career options out there. What is so significant about a job that people would choose to spend 40 or more hours a week working?

My significance for Pursue the Passion was generated from two painful experiences. The first was not having an answer to the question 'What should I do with my life?' when I graduated college. It was painful to not know the answer to that question, as it is for thousands of grads entering the workforce every year. The second experience was waking up every day and spending my life at a job that wasn't for me.

As we traveled around the country, the significance behind Pursue the Passion only grew. At every gas station and city sidewalk we had people pounding down on our RV door looking for a way out of their jobs. We spoke to student audiences who were looking for answers to their own 'What should I do with my life?' dilemmas. As we tacked on miles, we had experiences that strongly supported the stat that half the workforce is unhappy in their work.

All of those experiences gave significance to the project beyond it being just a road trip.

Significance gives people a sense of purpose in their job. From that purpose comes passion. This is especially important because every job you'll work will have elements that make it difficult to deal with at times. By knowing what the mission is, all the other stuff that you don't enjoy as much takes a backseat to what really matters.

Our interviewees were clued into a grand vision of why, day after day, they do the work that is important to them. By knowing the answer to 'why this job?' our interviewees not only found their passion, but were able to sustain it.

Redwood Forest, CA

TRAVELING NURSE I enjoy helping bring a new life into this world.

DOCUMENTARIAN Our country is at war, and I have to do my part as far as what I think is right. I feel like my part for what I can do with my privileges and my skills is to help Iraqis tell their stories. It's important work.

INTERIOR DESIGNER I'm motivated by what each project brings. I love going to work every day and feeling accomplished by seeing a project go from the drawing board to real life.

PUBLIC DEFENDER You feel for these kids. Every time you pick up a case, it's not just a fact set or legal issues. It's about a kid. It's about a family. Something went wrong, but are you going to exasperate the problem and make it worse for the kid and society as a whole? Or are you going to try make it better? Make this kid's life just slightly better. That's why I'm a public defender.

INSURANCE AGENT I love what I do because I get to be the hero. I get to be the solution. When someone gets in an accident, the doctor tells them they have a problem. Their lawyer outlines their problem for them. The banker is going to tell them they've got the problem. Well guess what? I'm the solution to their problems, because I'm the one with the checkbook. I get to be their hero when I cut their check, instead of the goat.

TATTOO ARTIST Someone is buying art from me, forever, on their body. That's way more of a complement than paying $50,000 for a black dot on a canvas.

HEDGE FUND MANAGER I would have days where I would upgrade a stock and the stock would go up 5%. I mean, that's a boost of adrenaline. You're like, 'Wow! The stock went up on my recommendation.'

CHILD THERAPIST I go home from work and can't believe I'm underpaid, underappreciated, all that stuff. But then I go into work the next day, and after I see that first kid, it's like, 'This is why I do this.'

HR MANAGER I have a chance to shape somebody's life. I have a chance to give people something that they have hoped for, but rarely found in regards to an ideal employment situation. If I can create that environment and that connection with them, I can see the excitement on their faces. I like to figure out a way to give excitement to them. That's what I love about Human Resources.

GENEALOGIST Families are forever. It's important to know where you come from. I help people realize the history behind their families. Without me, you might not know that your great Grandfather was a fish peddler during the Great Depression when he moved his wife and three daughters to Oakland to start a new life.

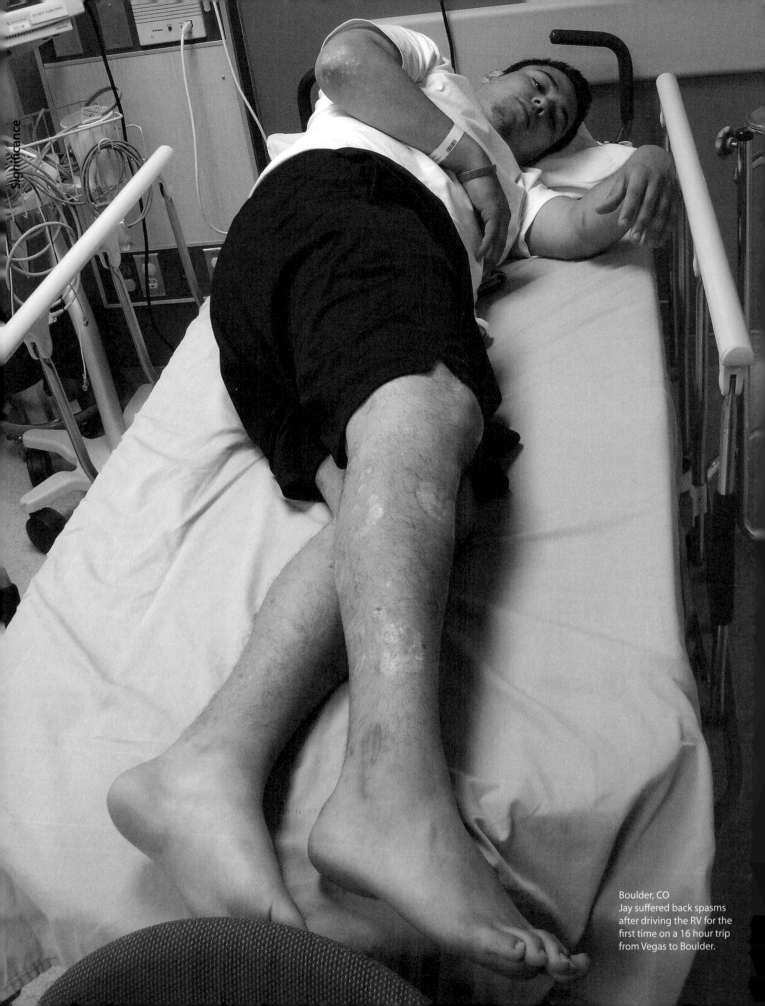

Boulder, CO
Jay suffered back spasms
after driving the RV for the
first time on a 16 hour trip
from Vegas to Boulder.

CARDIOVASCULAR TECHNOLOGIST My job is great fun. I enjoy it immensely. One of the most gratifying things is when you get a call from someone in the emergency room having a heart attack and they come down here, thriving in pain and sweating profusely. Sometimes they're gray in skin color. And they're really uncomfortable.

Our goal is when you get someone like that, is that in thirty minutes or less, have gone down and cleared the blockage, inflate the balloon, and stop the heart attack. It's really shocking to see a person come in like that. When we close the chest up, they stop sweating. Their color turns normal. They feel a lot better. Often times they feel normal again. And they ask if they can leave now. People actually ask if they can leave. You have to explain to them that they just had a heart attack so they have to stay in the hospital a couple days.

I think the best part about what we do here is that you can see immediate impact.

Especially with those people who are having a heart attack. They come in sick. We relieve their coronary. Thirty minutes later they're better. They're going to live happily ever after. Granny's out there in the lobby going 'Thank you! Thank you!' You really get the sense that you made a big difference for someone. That will make you passionate about what you do. There's nothing better when you give someone back to their family.

NON PROFIT DIRECTOR It's a great inspiration to be engaged in a mission, where every day when you come to work, you know exactly what you're working for.

HIGH SCHOOL PRINCIPAL The reason why I do my job is that the future of our country is at stake. If we sit on our laurels, the youth will not be prepared enough. The world is very competitive now. We need to make sure that our students are well trained. That's the right reason to be in education.

REAL ESTATE DEVELOPER What I like is to find property that's vacant and build something out of it. I enjoy seeing people use it. For our company, its senior housing. You take a vacant piece of property, you build something, and you see some older folks who come in and appreciate it. You're creating a home for them. A home that feeds them, takes care of them. That's pretty rewarding to see that happen.

It's more rewarding to build something that you can see when you're done, versus working at a grocery store. Which I did. You put things on a shelf and they're gone at the end of the day. You do that for fifty years, where all you do is put things on a shelf and you can't stand back and look at your work and see you've created something.

COMMERCIAL REAL ESTATE AGENT I feel responsible to do my part in rebuilding the New York economy after the 9/11 strike.

EVENT PLANNER On Singles Night we sell these packages for $25 that includes a ticket to the game, one drink coupon, and entrance to the pre-game party. We bring DJ's, do contests and turn our corporate picnic area into a huge dance floor. It's like throwing a big party.

The other day I sent out this big email blast about Singles Night to our past clients. This lady called me back and asked me to take her off the mailing list. I'm like 'Sure, do you mind if I ask why?' She told me she got married from someone she met at Singles Night. It's sounds cliché, but that's almost magical. We've had six people get married through our Singles Night. I got a wedding invitation once from some guy. Those are the things that I won't be able to accomplish and experience working for a mortgage company.

St. Charles, MO

DRUG MANUFACTURER In manufacturing, you work hard and you make these products, but you don't see it at the end of the day. I wasn't in the final fill where you put it in a vial, you put in a box, and you ship it out. You have these big stainless tanks and all this equipment, and as much as work as you're doing towards a final product, your real work is making it and documenting it.

But I really like the fact that we're doing something that at the end of the day derives a benefit for folks. Especially from the perspective that I've had my own family members who have taken our products. Being able to see that perspective, where they go from one day feeling really cruddy to the next day doing things that they haven't been able to do in years, that really is the bonus. When you see the impact on them, it makes the work significant.

Seattle, WA

PHYSICAL THERAPIST Everyone has their own thing that will motivate them. I think the secret to motivating somebody is really finding out what's important to them.

VOICEOVER AGENT Allowing actors to make enough money so that they can pursue their theatrical aspirations gives me a great deal of professional satisfaction. Building someone's career. Taking people who had real jobs and have real families and kids to feed, and taking them from earning $60k a year to $580k a year. Allowing them to focus 100% of their time on voiceover. That to me is the goal.

RESTAURANT MANAGER I find the most inspiration from nature. What cooking is for us is representing what food is from nature to the plate. We're messengers that take it from a form here, and take it to a form that's recognizable and done to the finest degree.

New York, NY

HEALTHCARE ENTREPRENEUR The ultimate vision we have is making a real difference in healthcare. In our little neck of the woods, it's a small niche in healthcare, but it's going to make a big difference in the quality of healthcare around the world. That helps crop some of the peaks and valleys experienced in a start up and allows us to maintain our sanity along the way.

MEDICAL RESEARCHER Mainly what I'm doing now is I'm writing a lot of reports. I do a lot of analysis to see what the information says.

All the things you might ignore, or care about.

But, it's fun and exciting because it has the potential to be really helpful to people. Because if our patients can use their hands, they can operate the wheelchair. They can work on the computer. They can interact with the world. It would do a lot for their quality of life.

REAL ESTATE INVESTOR # I have to tell you that this job can be very frustrating.

You do all the work on a deal. You do all the analysis, the research in the market, you fly into all the stores, you take pictures of all the stores, you're working like a dog. You make a bid, and then someone else outbids you. You spend all this money and time, and you have zero. A big goose egg to show for it.

I figured that if I kept at it, eventually I would find an acquisition that would fall through the net, and I would end up with a chain. The prospect of that big payoff is what keeps me going.

CAREER COACH One of the things that propels me is the agony of other people looking for jobs. That desperation and anguish. Say you've had a job for 27 years and your company lays you off. You haven't had to interview for a job in 27 years. That's really scary. Plus, your rent still needs to get paid.

I'd like to help people be confident in who they are in whatever they're looking to get into.

The Freeway

Cape Cod, MA

115

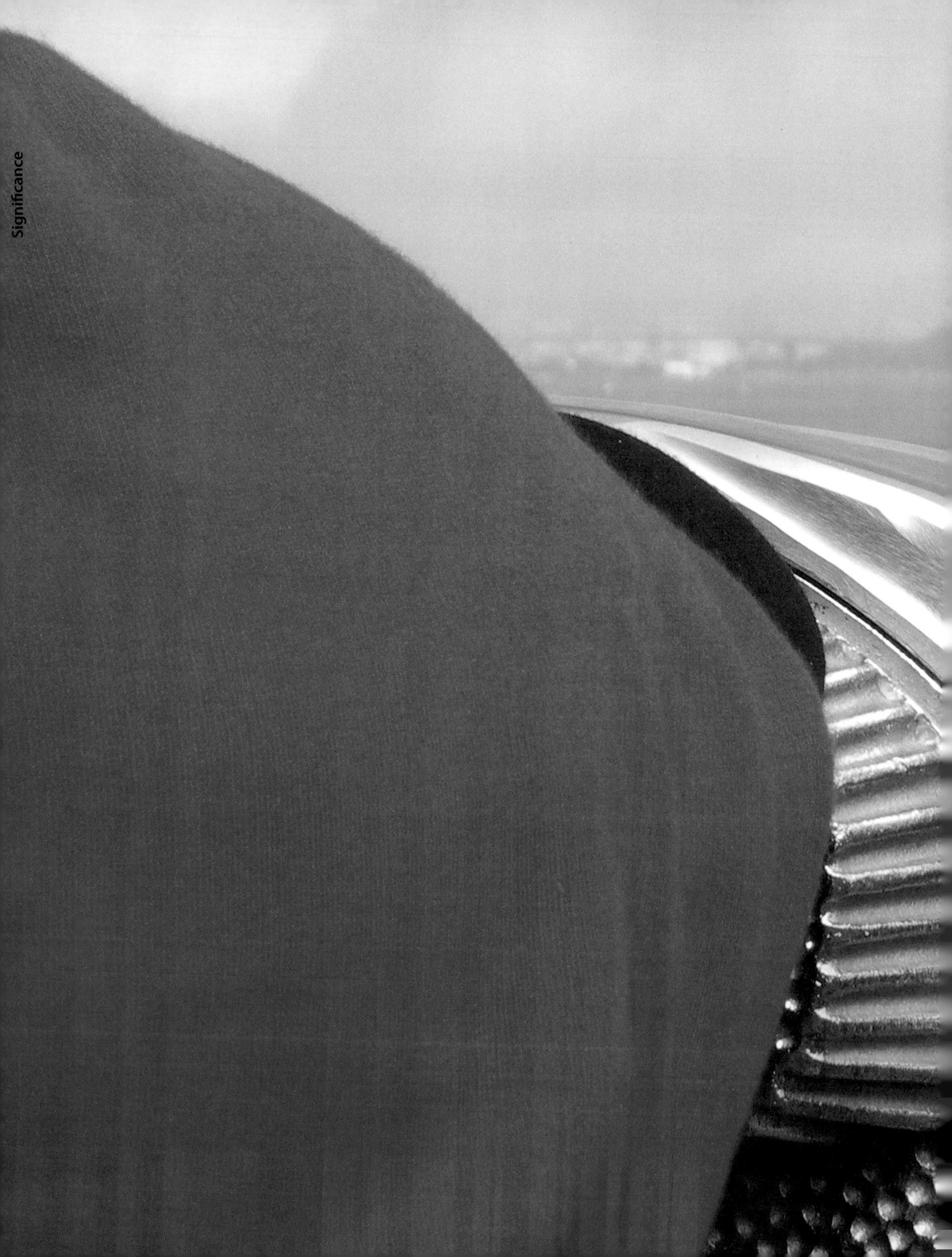

SERIAL ENTREPRENEUR If you're just looking to be an entrepreneur and get rich, or looking to be successful, that's not very motivating every day.

In the end, that's a nice end point to be at. Sure, I'd like to sell a company and make a million. But, it's hard to get there and if you don't enjoy doing the grunt work, you won't get there.

I'm sort of a harebrain guy. I tried to start so many companies. I have a list of just wacky ideas. A lot of those ideas sort of fizzled out. It's not that they failed, but it's like a couple months later I was wondering why I was doing it. You get some perspective on what you're doing and you realize it's kind of stupid. So you peter out.

We definitely felt like doing this idea was worth it even if it was not successful. If no one else knew about it, and it was just us, we would have done it. The actual content of the idea I enjoy every day. I actually enjoy working in Africa. I enjoy all the people I was meeting. I enjoy the purpose and cared for it, in and of itself.

The thing that kept us going was the actual work, we liked. Rather than the result. And that's the difference.

FROZEN CUSTARD RETAILERS We're in the business of creating memories. I remember when I was a kid growing up, my grandfather would take trips to the city to pick up the Chicago Tribune and an ice cream cone for me. Two square scoops on a cake cone and then it we'd take it to the tracks and watch the trains go by. Forty years later, I still hold on to those memories.

That's what we do here in this neighborhood. We create memories with frozen custard. People gather here to meet with their neighbors and talk at the tables outside. The neighborhood kids ride their bikes to our shop and grow up together here.

The memory business. It's a great business to be in.

MARKETING CONSULTANT My sister used to say, 'There's a lot of bullshit in every job.' I took that and extrapolated that to, 'The key is to find a job that you love so much, that you don't mind putting up with the bullshit.'

There's always going to be some part of the job you don't like. If you're passionate about it, and you love it, and everything else is going well, you don't mind the part that isn't.

I love to get with business people and talk business and help them make the breakthroughs. Getting someone to have a breakthrough is what I'm all about. Do I love getting on a plane, and leaving my family, and going on the other side of the planet, and waiting in airports, and eating bad food? No. I hate all that. But why do I do it? Because I love the other part so much, that I don't mind that part of it.

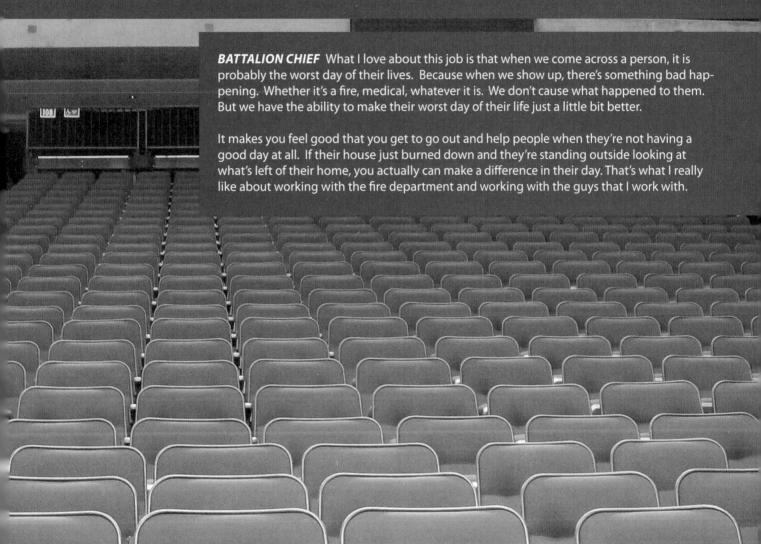

BASKETBALL EXECUTIVE My greatest thrill is walking into an arena filled with 18,000 people and watching it all unfold. I can't control what happens on the court. I can control how people feel about the experience of being there. For me, that's where the passion really comes from.

BATTALION CHIEF What I love about this job is that when we come across a person, it is probably the worst day of their lives. Because when we show up, there's something bad happening. Whether it's a fire, medical, whatever it is. We don't cause what happened to them. But we have the ability to make their worst day of their life just a little bit better.

It makes you feel good that you get to go out and help people when they're not having a good day at all. If their house just burned down and they're standing outside looking at what's left of their home, you actually can make a difference in their day. That's what I really like about working with the fire department and working with the guys that I work with.

Houston, TX

119

RADIO VOICE Waking up at 4 in the morning…that part of my job is not fun. But I'm going to see more great music than a lot of people. I'm going to get paid to talk about music, and expose people to the types of music I like. That's all I want.

SOCIAL ACTIVIST I don't always stay positive. There's a lot of tears in my work. I recognize that my work begins with suffering. I get inspiration from the women who have survived abuse and are really working to complete their healing. From the men who take a stand to be non violent in their home. From the children who amazingly bounce back from these family experiences. That's what motivates me to work. It's not always a pleasant experience.

DONATION ADVOCATE There are almost a hundred thousand people on the waiting list. They keep me going. All the people who are on the waiting list really feel like their life is on pause. Those people are an inspiration to me. They make me want to help raise awareness and get people to say yes to a donation.

ART DIRECTOR There are days where the grunt work is 70% of what I'm doing. It's really important then to keep in mind what's really meaningful. Because our perceptions can be so clouded by what's recent. You forget that two days ago some really cool thing happened that is showing you the impact you're having on an organization. Your own sense of productivity is not just how much money you're making or how many sales you're booking, but that part of it that's a real payback.

LEGAL ADVOCATE The work is…on some days it's insanely frustrating. I hate it and I want to go home. I can't stand it. Getting through the tougher times…I haven't really developed a strategy for it. I don't have a general approach. It's sort of on a case by case basis.

Sometimes it's finding strength from the people who live here. I think about my position and how privileged I am to be a part of it and volunteer. I'm here on my own accord and I'm not a disaster victim. I'm an American citizen who wants to stand with people who were knocked down by decades of racism in the South of the United States.

I came down here to be with people and stand with people who have problems. It's not even about my issues. I try to move on from it when it feels that way by getting in touch with why I'm here in the first place.

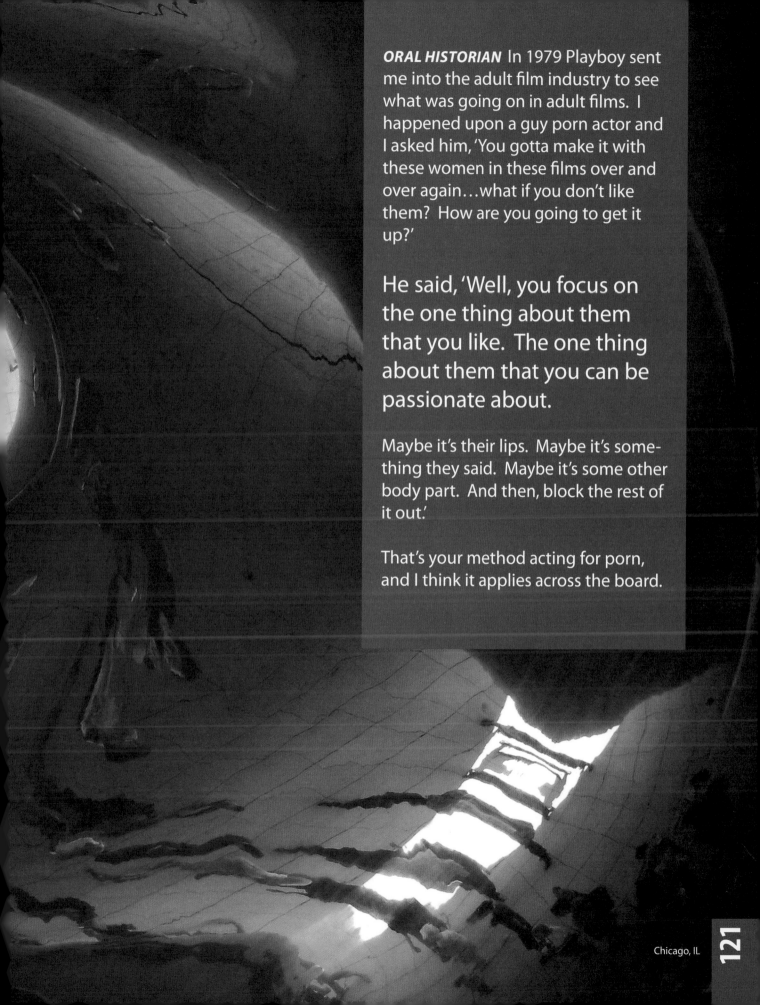

ORAL HISTORIAN In 1979 Playboy sent me into the adult film industry to see what was going on in adult films. I happened upon a guy porn actor and I asked him, 'You gotta make it with these women in these films over and over again…what if you don't like them? How are you going to get it up?'

He said, 'Well, you focus on the one thing about them that you like. The one thing about them that you can be passionate about.

Maybe it's their lips. Maybe it's something they said. Maybe it's some other body part. And then, block the rest of it out.'

That's your method acting for porn, and I think it applies across the board.

REPORTER I lived Hurricane Katrina. The most memorable story was the night before it happened.

As everyone was evacuating, all these people came to the Mississippi Coliseum to sleep on a hard floor. The Red Cross had set up a shelter there, very last minute, and there were 15,000 people in there. These people were the worst of the worst. They were the poorest. They didn't have cars. They came in buses. They didn't have a lot of belongings. They were in wheelchairs. These were the last people to leave New Orleans. They didn't have cots. They didn't have blankets. They didn't have pillows. They didn't have toothpaste. Anything like that.

We went there and everyone is sleeping on the cold concrete floor in this place. We interviewed them. The Sheriff was out there calling for people to come help because these people had nothing. Within thirty minutes of the broadcast I did, there were, I would say 1,000 people outside. Volunteers from Mississippi coming and bringing in sleeping bags, mattresses, blankets, pillows, toothpaste. The pictures are unbelievable of the amount of donations that came in. And that was literally 15-20 minutes after signing off from that location that they came. It was amazing. That was awesome.

It only took one minute of TV to get that kind of reaction. One minute of the Sheriff saying the place was a disaster and requesting help. And boom, there it was.

If there's anything that's going to make you passionate, in this business, that's the kind of stuff that will do it.

New Orleans, LA

123

ASTROLOGER Question what you're doing and see if it helps the world. I believe that asking yourself whether there is any validity to what I'm doing is important for anyone. Doctors should do that, lawyers should to that, astrologers should to that. Everyone should to that. Question yourself about what you do has any validity at all to making the world a better place. If I don't ask that question, I'm not humble enough. I try to ask that question every day.

PR FIRM PARTNER There's people who think that what they're doing is rocket science and is going to change the world when it's not. I recognize that what we do, public relations, is important for our client's image and reputation. But is it going to end world hunger? No. Is it going to bring peace to Iraq? No it's not. So you have to take that in perspective.

PIZZA SHOP OWNER It's more than just selling pizzas. It's being a good fit for the community. It's a betterment of the community as much as anything.

RELOCATION DIRECTOR I'm not a big religious person, but I believe I'm in Chicago to do this job. Absolutely. I would say that every day we get to move families into housing, it's exciting. Because we have families that have lived for forty years in a high rise building that wasn't taken care of. There's no better joy than when a family like that has gotten a job, gotten their kids in childcare, and made a decision to really make a change in their life.

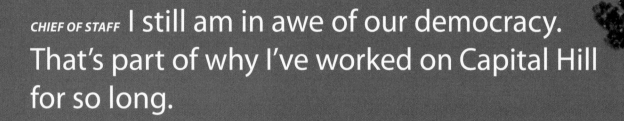

CHIEF OF STAFF I still am in awe of our democracy. That's part of why I've worked on Capital Hill for so long.

We're debating really important issues and making really big decisions for the country here on Capital Hill. The members are, and we as staff are helping them.

I think a lot of us are here because we have passionate views about a lot of these issues. We care very much about the policies of our country and the priorities they represent. Our roads, the quality of our air, the schools our kids go to. So many of the decisions that are made here affect our lives. We're driven by the values that we have, and want to bring those values to the discussions within our government.

CHIEF OF INFRASTRUCTURE If you look at America and people's everyday's lives, from the moment they wake up to the moment they go to bed, their lives are touched by infrastructure in so many different ways so often. You ask yourself, 'If I build this road, it's going to make so and so's life much easier because they can get to work faster or their kids can cross the street.'

It might only affect a single person or maybe a small constituency like a neighborhood. But you start to quickly see that even though government tends to be big and a little on the slow side, and not always glamorous, it does have tremendous impact when it focuses on a cradle to grave type of process.

It's way cool.

Madison, WI

125

YOUTH PROGRAM DIRECTOR I went to school close to Cabrini. The grammar school I went to had a lot of kids from public housing areas. I had no idea that I was the only white kid in class or that these kids were from public housing because it was an art school. Everyone did dance, drama, music, piano, and art. It was great.

The kids who experienced success in the classroom were some of the best dancers or actors and they felt very proud of themselves. I never realized it at the time, but when I first started teaching I looked back at my experience as a kid in grammar school and saw the benefits that these kids received from having that boost of programming. Math didn't make them feel great. Reading didn't make them feel great. But dancing? Or drama? Or in our case, soccer? That makes these kids feel great about themselves.

We figure if we give kids a reason to get up and get to the classroom, they'll do it. We've seen results. We get close to thirty kids out in the mornings before school to play soccer. If it's pouring rain, these kids will still show up because they love it so much. That's the concept behind it. Get them to buy into something beyond school, and then tie it back into the classroom.

HOTEL MANAGER Typically people look at an overnight position as a role where no one sees you. Or you think you don't have any value to the property. I look at it just the opposite.

One of my mentors was my manager when I was the overnight security guard. He was one of those people who said you either learn how you want to do stuff, or you learn how you don't want to do stuff. He was one of the guys who showed me exactly how I wanted to do stuff.

Once a week I'd walk in after my night shift and give him his report because he wanted it fresh off the presses. And he'd say, 'Do understand what you just did tonight?' Then he'd walk me through it so I understood how important this report was, and how important it was to him to make decisions. That gave my job a lot of meaning.

New Orleans, LA

127

CARTOONIST There was a guy I met who was an accountant. Accounting is one of those jobs, me coming from an artistic background, it's like, that job must suck. So I asked him about it.

He said, 'When I think about it, when I was a kid I used to watch the old westerns that were black and white. There would be the guys in the white hats, who were the good guys, and then the guys in the black hats. They'd fight against each other. Now that I'm a CPA, I help young families and couples. I look at myself as the guy in the white hat, and the IRS are the guys in the black hat. My job is to help them keep as much of their money as they can and help them out.'

Badlands, SD

TASTEMASTER The best flavor of ice cream I've created is the one where the person puts it in their mouth, and their eyes close, and they go, 'Oh my gosh that's so good.' That first bite is what I live for.

When they take that first bite and it's heaven to them, it doesn't matter what the flavor is. They're enjoying something that I made. That gives me pleasure. That's really where it's at for me. That's why I get passionate about ice cream.

GRAPHIC DESIGNER I design the Phoenix Suns program with the stats and stuff that they hand out at the game. I love the fact that the stuff I'm putting together goes out and is viewed by thousands of people. And that happens every night at the Suns game.

HUMANITARIAN It's really exciting when I go out to the places where we have programs and see that we're changing people's lives in very tangible ways. People can talk about what it's meant to them and their families to participate in the programs that CARE supports. It's just inspiring. That's what keeps me inspired.

SPORTS MARKETER When I was an intern I was responsible for picking out clothes to give to magazines for their models to wear. When I got the magazine back I saw the outfit I picked out was on the cover. I took pride in the fact that something I picked out was published.

CIRCUS LADY Eleven of my advanced students from all different backgrounds went to Israel and worked with these Jewish and Arab children. One of the first shows we did was at a home for people with cerebral palsy. I about burst into tears. These kids, who didn't know each other before, were putting together this inspirational show for these people who hardly ever get to leave home and sharing that energy, enthusiasm, and that love for circus. It was really magical to see that, and it's why I do what I do.

STAFFING FIRM CEO There's a few things that can effect people in their life. Marriage, divorce, relocation, job change, having children. We get to play a role in one of the five biggest things in someone's life.

ORGANIST What's great about being here is that I've always enjoyed the music being played at the baseball games. Kids in their 20's, who you would think like rock n' roll, enjoy the organ because they're at a ballgame. You'd think they'd listen to their iPod while they're watching the game, but they're not. I get to provide them with songs like Take Me Out to The Ballgame.

WEDDING PHOTOGRAPHER You can be the best photographer in the world, but if no one sees your photos, does it matter?

129

Significance

ENTREPRENEURSHIP EXPERT I think that the American Dream is that if we work hard enough, if we're smart enough, that we're going to get there. We're going to be almost guaranteed financial return. But it just doesn't work that way. Most of us don't quite get to the pot of gold at the end of the rainbow.

You know, my family last year, we did the bridge climb in Sydney, Australia. We actually saw a 270 degree rainbow when we got to the top of that bridge. And you know something? There was no pot of gold at the end of that 270 degree rainbow. There was just a beautiful view with your family.

And maybe that's what it's about.

DOCTOR It doesn't have to be big and fancy. But, if it's got the passion, and it's got the meaning, it naturally gets done.

131

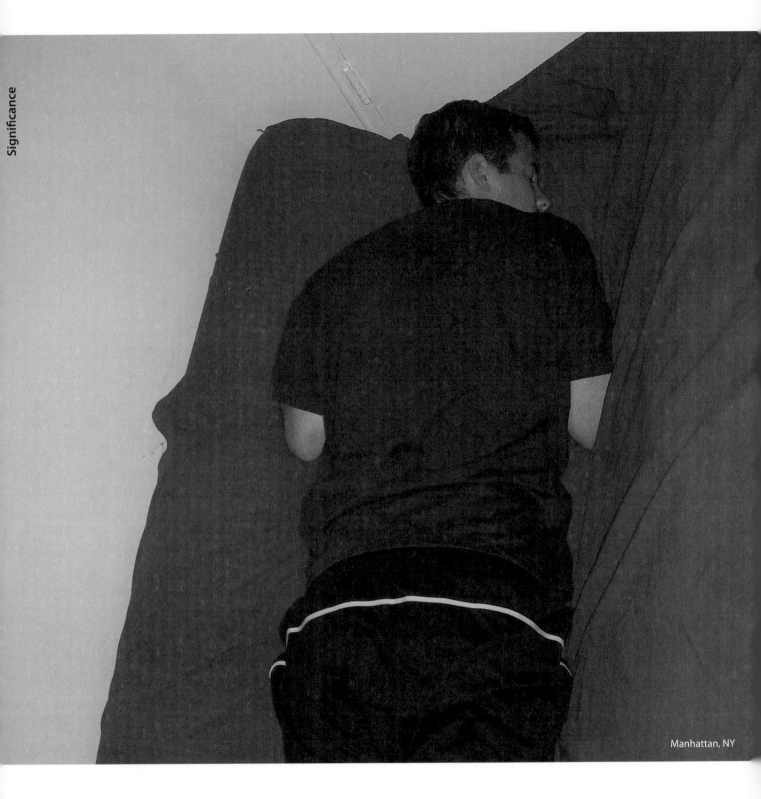

Manhattan, NY

THAT GUY It's like, what gets you up in the morning? You know?

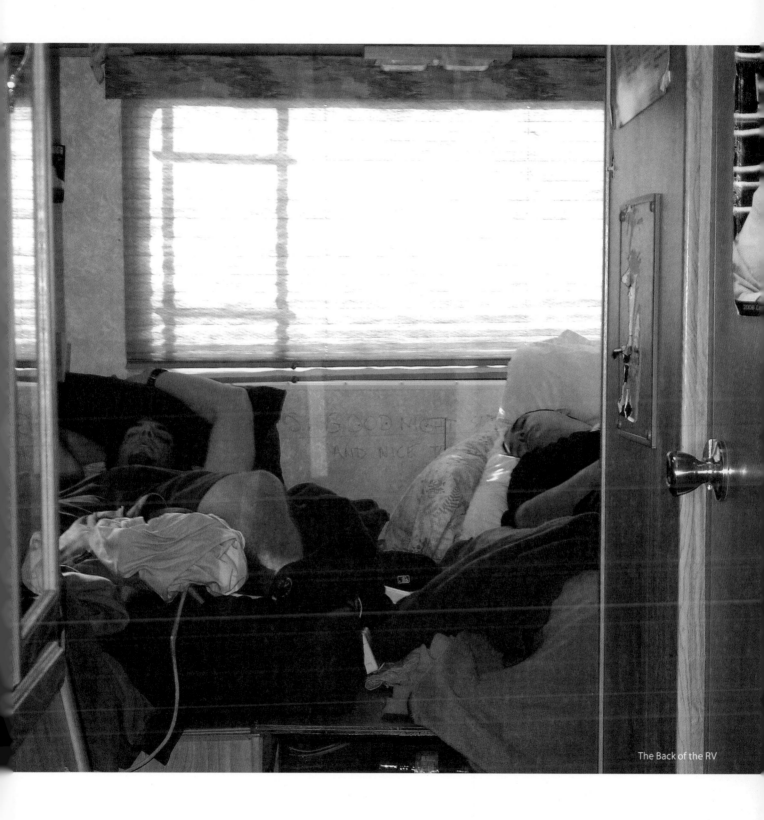

The Back of the RV

There's a lot of respect for managers who give you a lot of rope. And with that rope you can swing around on or you can hang yourself. But it's you who are responsible for making one of those two things happen.

HR MANAGER

I was lucky that I had a guy like Steve Wynn, who gave all the support you can imagine. He believed that Human Resources wasn't a thing we had to do, it was a thing that ran our business. He kept supporting me in the ideas I had, and I kept running to achieve the goals that he had. And together, we were very, very, very successful.

Roll the Credits: P204

Trust

People want to be trusted to do the job they were hired to do.

When I think about trust, I think about how Jobing.com entrusted four college grads with a 30 foot RV and enough cash to get around the country. What's significant is that Jobing didn't tell us how to do our project. They didn't tell us who to interview, where to go, or who to stay with. When we would approach them with questions, they would ask a question of their own: 'How do you think it should be done?' Jobing simply trusted us to do things our way in order to create something great.

Unfortunately, trust is one of the most absent elements from work. It's hard to earn it from an employee perspective, and it's hard to award it from a manager perspective. But it's an absolute essential.

Without trust, no one works at full capacity. Not the manager, not the employee, not the company. When an employee operates in a trusting environment, there is the potential to go beyond the status quo and complete work that is above expectations.

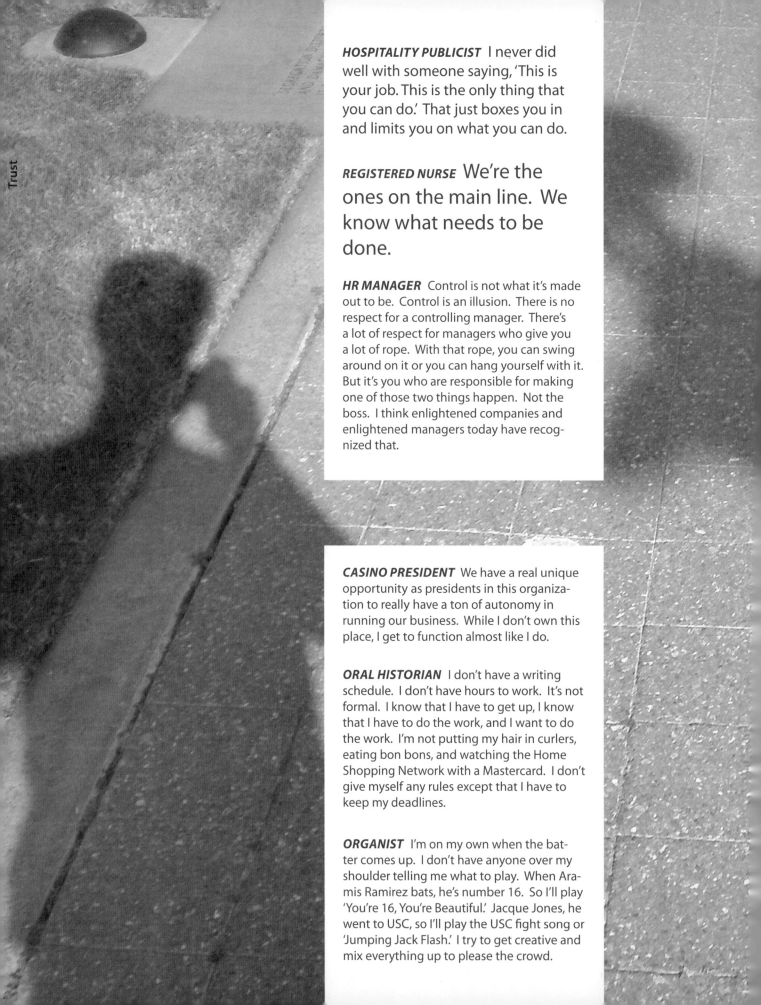

HOSPITALITY PUBLICIST I never did well with someone saying, 'This is your job. This is the only thing that you can do.' That just boxes you in and limits you on what you can do.

REGISTERED NURSE We're the ones on the main line. We know what needs to be done.

HR MANAGER Control is not what it's made out to be. Control is an illusion. There is no respect for a controlling manager. There's a lot of respect for managers who give you a lot of rope. With that rope, you can swing around on it or you can hang yourself with it. But it's you who are responsible for making one of those two things happen. Not the boss. I think enlightened companies and enlightened managers today have recognized that.

CASINO PRESIDENT We have a real unique opportunity as presidents in this organization to really have a ton of autonomy in running our business. While I don't own this place, I get to function almost like I do.

ORAL HISTORIAN I don't have a writing schedule. I don't have hours to work. It's not formal. I know that I have to get up, I know that I have to do the work, and I want to do the work. I'm not putting my hair in curlers, eating bon bons, and watching the Home Shopping Network with a Mastercard. I don't give myself any rules except that I have to keep my deadlines.

ORGANIST I'm on my own when the batter comes up. I don't have anyone over my shoulder telling me what to play. When Aramis Ramirez bats, he's number 16. So I'll play 'You're 16, You're Beautiful.' Jacque Jones, he went to USC, so I'll play the USC fight song or 'Jumping Jack Flash.' I try to get creative and mix everything up to please the crowd.

VENTURE CAPITALIST The worst thing a VC can do to an entrepreneur is show up every week and spend a day in the office. I'm an early stage entrepreneur and I hear lots of people say, 'We love to spend real face time with our entrepreneurs.' That's good. I spend lots of face time with the people I fund and work with.

But if you go and spend a day a week, you can almost guarantee that the day before is going to be spent thinking and preparing for that meeting. The day after will be spent doing random things that came out of that meeting. You basically are cutting your focused work time in half in the aggregate. You lose two or three days out of a six day work week.

Do you really want that investor all over you, all the time?

PHYSICAL THERAPIST Trust is very, very important if you want to see results. I think we spend our entire first treatment building that trust.

Chicago, IL

HR MANAGER I don't know if you remember the first time you rode a bike. The first time your father lets go of the bike, and you don't know it. All of a sudden you discover that, and then you think, 'Wow. I'm doing this on my own.' And you get all excited. You see that look on a kid's face, and you see that look on employee's faces when they get in that same kind of employment situation.

Trust

THERAPEUTIC HORSE TRAINER

If you are in the business world, regardless of whether you have the word 'manager' attached to your title, you will have a boss.

OUTPLACEMENT MANAGER
People always want to be an entrepreneur and be their own boss. They don't realize there's always a boss somewhere. You take your company public and the shareholders are your boss. You get some venture capital and the venture capitalists are your boss. You have to serve your clients and they become the boss. Even growing up, your parents are the boss.

There's always a boss somewhere.

THERAPEUTIC HORSE TRAINER

The unfortunate thing about managers is that sometimes they want to be the toughest person in the room. Because they believe they're the #1 person, they act like they're the number one person. But that's not always the case.

On our farm we've got ten horses all corralled within this area. We have one horse in particular that walks around like he owns the place. He bullies the other horses, and kind of acts tough. Now these horses have an unspoken ranking system amongst each other, much like the business world. The horse I'm referring to believes he's the number one horse, he acts like the number one horse, but really, he's around the four or five horse.

Now how many managers in the world think they're this number one horse?

They act tough, they boss people around, but really, they're not even the number one horse. Managers have to be aware that respect, and trust, and treating people the way they're supposed to be treated is what will move them up the ranks. Because then people will want to work for you and give their best effort.

Burt, NY

PIZZA SHOP OWNER The industry standard is a one year turnover. Which means if I have 15 people working here, I'd have another 15 people in less than a year. Most of the people who have been working with me have been here for three, four, five years. We've got some who have been here longer than that.

In order for myself or this business to be successful, I have to have like minded individuals that want to make it successful. The best way that I've found to do that is to empower them to represent the business as if it was their own. Make the decisions. We give them some bylaws that they have to attain. We give them minimum goals that they have to attain. And anything from that, it's their own flair and character. That's what makes it fun to come in.

Employees, they should feel comfortable. They should feel like they belong in here. They'll keep coming back. They'll rely on each other. And they don't need me in the midst of this. Because then what am I? I'm a boss! I don't want to be a boss. I don't want to be that guy. That's not why we're here. We're all adults. Manage your lives. You don't need me to do that for you.

Spokane, WA

AUTHOR The person you work for is going to make a huge difference on how you feel about your job. For a lot of reasons. That's something to really think about. You may say you hate your job or your career, but do you really hate your career, or is it just your job? Should you look for a new company, or would you work for someone different?

LIFE COACH I've found that many people who were feeling like they weren't connected to their passions, who weren't happy, who weren't able to speak their truth in a corporate environment.

The reason is, a lot of the time in corporate setting, people don't feel like they can speak their truth. There's all kinds of connections and connotations that we have when we think about it. If people really know how I feel, somehow I'll be vulnerable and exposed. There's something that's very powerful about it, and that's why it's scary.

But in corporate America, if you really speak your truth, you're probably not going to last very long. What I find with a lot of the people I work with, some ten, fifteen, twenty years in the workforce, they have been continually choking down their voice. Really what they've been doing is extinguishing their fire.

That's troubling, because that shuts down any enthusiasm you would have for developing a vision. But when you feel trusted, that's when everything opens up. And that's where you can create whatever you want, like a cross country tour with a beautiful new RV.

TASTEMASTER The great thing about Cold Stone is that no matter what flavor I develop, everyone will listen to me. I'm trusted. No matter how strange or out of the box the idea is, they're always receptive to it. Some ideas will make it to market and some won't. But no matter what, there's always room in the pantry.

MUSIC PRODUCER We make sure that when another drummer comes in, that everything they need to do their thing is all taken care of. Nothing gets in the way. That's important. Because then that creative person can really achieve their best potential.

I just like removing those roadblocks and trying to make it seamless and smooth for people. It's more about enabling other people to do stuff. It's about making this a place where creative people can do amazing things.

ANIMATOR When I started at Disney it was a depressing place. *Black Caldren* was crap and there were all these old guys in there that weren't interested in making new films. Tim Burton was there at the time. Tim wanted to do all this really cool stuff and the old guys were like, 'You don't know how to draw.' They stuck him a corner somewhere. They weren't appreciating all these ideas.

SCREENWRITER I loved Roger Korman films when I was a kid. He made these great drive in movies. He was a bright guy, made a lot of money doing it. He would hire interesting and up and coming film makers. Coppola, Scorsese, all these guys. He'd give them a non existent budget, but enough to make a movie. A couple of cheesy actors and a concept. All they had to do was give him his marketable elements. 'I need tits on page 8, 18, and 36. I need something to blow up here, and I need a dragon. Go make a movie.'

These guys would go out and make movies that were insanely inventive and fun. But the straight to video world is not that way. They're dour and nervous about the market and what the audience wants, more so than studio executives are. They're terrified of anything that isn't proven. They want to do a movie just like the last 800 they sold. And if you try to do something innovative or weird they get very nervous and anxious. Which is too bad, because that should be a fun world.

In one straight to video movie I wrote up this car chase. You'd never seen a car chase like this in a film. It was an angle that had never been done. I put this in the script and when I saw the film the director didn't use it. So I took it out of that script and put it into the one Paramount bought. It was actually one of their favorite things. There's a really important lesson there.

Cape Cod, MA

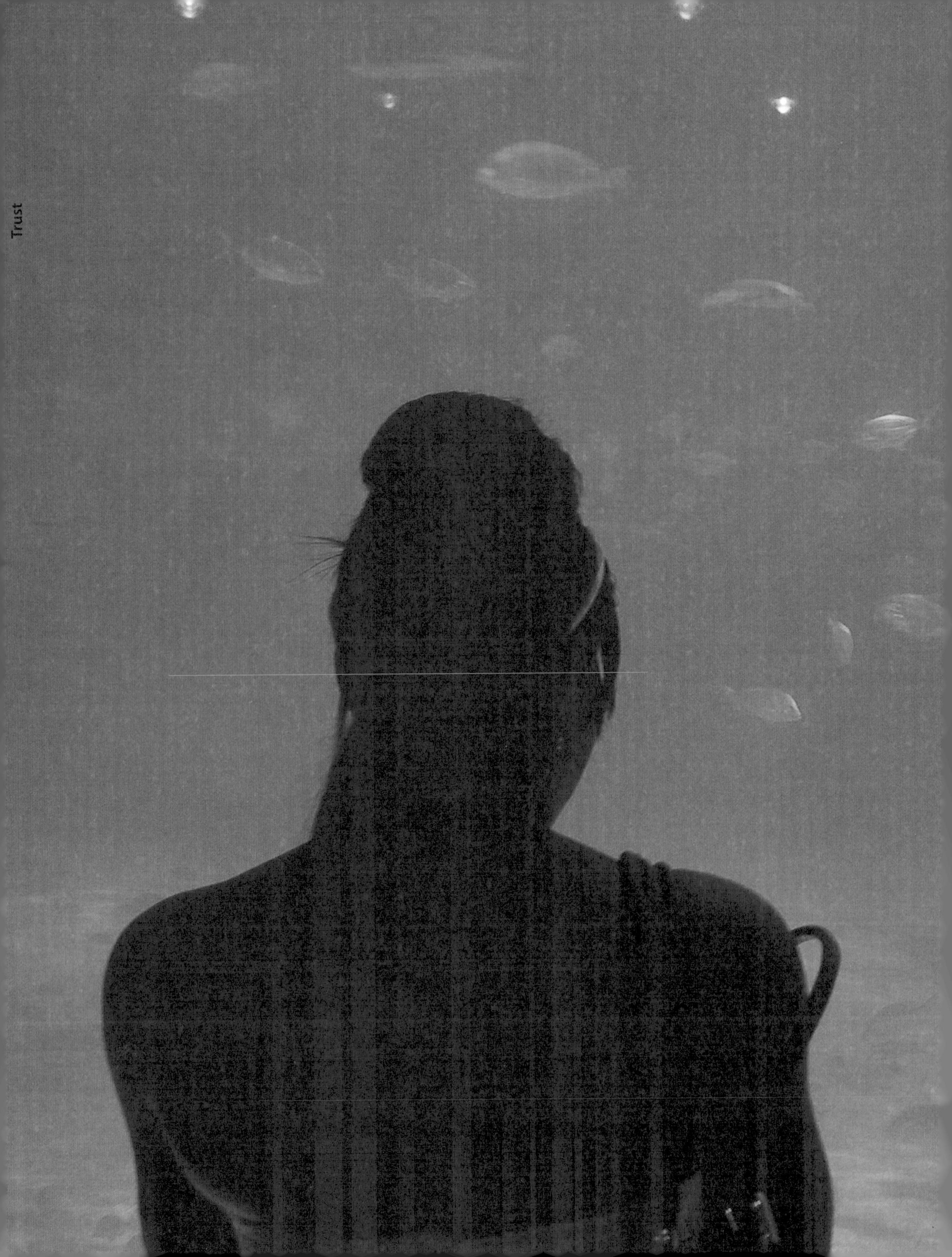

GOAT FARMER If you're going to pursue your passion, you need to find someone who supports that passion. That's a difficult thing. A lot of people figure out what their passion is, but they're in a life situation where the other person involved, or the company involved isn't on board with that.

PR FIRM PARTNER I mean, if you have the wrong mate that doesn't support and trust you in your pursuit, there's no way it's going to happen. Having that person there is not only an emotional support, but understands financially that it's going to be really tough for a year or so. That makes all the difference in the world. My wife is what got me through it. She said to not worry about the money and that'd we'd get by and we'd succeed. That was big.

CELEBRITY CHEF There are times where you have to say to the person, 'Could you just do that? Don't look at me and worry about it. Just do it. And if you burn it and it's screwed up and lands on the floor, then we'll talk about it.' That's my attitude.

GUITAR SCHOOL INSTRUCTOR We want a place where everyone is hard working. We want a place where everyone is respectful. Where everyone is sincere. Where everyone takes out the garbage that needs to be taken out. Where everyone cleans and does a good job cleaning the bathroom.

The only way to achieve all those things is if you have a trusting culture. Because then you don't have to micromanage. I know that Jen and Morgan are over there doing things their way. It may not be my way, but if it's with the culture, then it's going to be done great.

SALES DIRECTOR For me, with our sales folks, the lesson is to get them as ready as you can. But eventually you have to kick them out of the nest and let them fly. That's the only way they can do it. Just getting on the phone and getting after it.

Atlanta, GA

EXECUTIVE TV PRODUCER The thing about trust is it leaves room for mistakes to be made. If you give too much trust too early, there's room that those mistakes might be high pro-file.

My biggest mistake was a really famous clip. Did you ever see *Bowling for Columbine*? There's a really famous clip where there's a pursuit in Los Angeles. At the end of the pursuit there's a big standoff. This guy takes a shotgun and blows his head off live on TV. And I was producing at KNBC that day in the control room when that happened.

I was kind of like, 'Oh wow that guy has a shotgun. Oh wow he stuck it in his mouth.' I was watching it instead of editing. So of course, that was huge. Instead of pulling out or going to black, that was the worst day of my career.

Overcoming it was largely due to bosses that didn't sell me out. They could have very easily gotten me fired. But they protected me from the onslaught. So it was learning from live TV and deciding what to do next time. What I did was I went to them and said, 'Alright. I messed up. Here's what I would have done differently for next time.'

That was the biggest mistake I've made. Pretty big one. Millions of people saw it and it's in a movie.

DRUG MANUFACTURER There is a tendency in a business setting when things go wrong, people start to blame. It usually starts with why did it go wrong? What happened? And then, who did it wrong? Oftentimes, I don't want to say a waste of time, but it's usually inappropriately done in the sense that at the beginning, you should make sure that everything gets fixed up and put back in place. From a lesson learned perspective, I absolutely see the value.

From a getting people in trouble perspective, I think it's important that you keep track of mistakes and who does them for a long term type of thing. Something we say here is that if you make a mistake, just don't do it again. It's the second and third times where it becomes an issue.

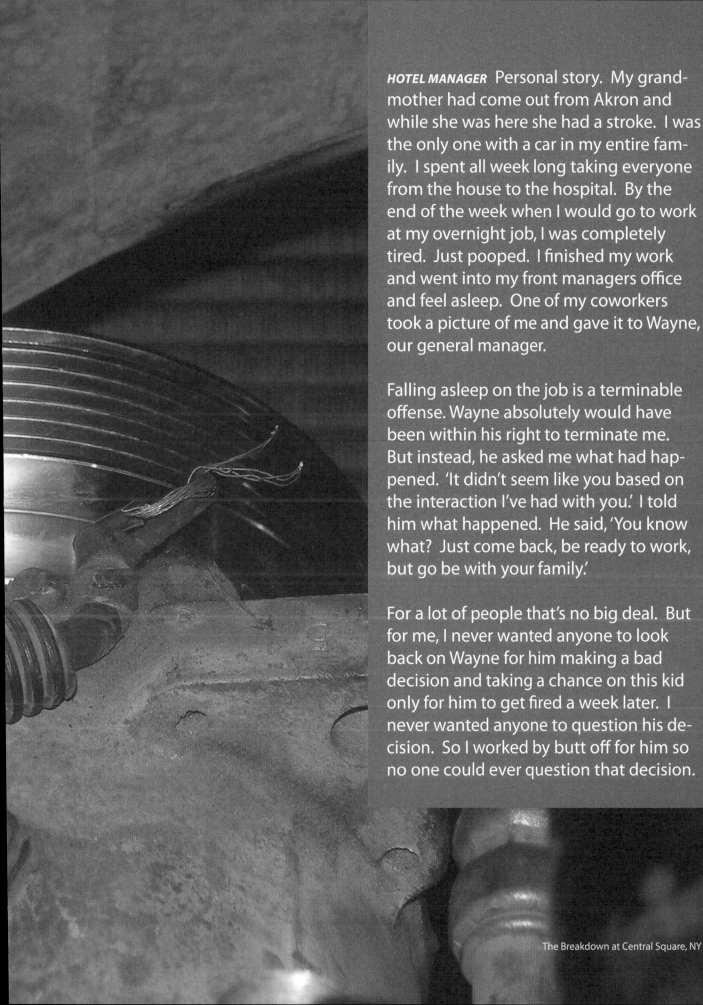

HOTEL MANAGER Personal story. My grandmother had come out from Akron and while she was here she had a stroke. I was the only one with a car in my entire family. I spent all week long taking everyone from the house to the hospital. By the end of the week when I would go to work at my overnight job, I was completely tired. Just pooped. I finished my work and went into my front managers office and feel asleep. One of my coworkers took a picture of me and gave it to Wayne, our general manager.

Falling asleep on the job is a terminable offense. Wayne absolutely would have been within his right to terminate me. But instead, he asked me what had happened. 'It didn't seem like you based on the interaction I've had with you.' I told him what happened. He said, 'You know what? Just come back, be ready to work, but go be with your family.'

For a lot of people that's no big deal. But for me, I never wanted anyone to look back on Wayne for him making a bad decision and taking a chance on this kid only for him to get fired a week later. I never wanted anyone to question his decision. So I worked by butt off for him so no one could ever question that decision.

REPORTER Putting a newscast on the air, one person can't do it. There's a huge team. You have to respect what everyone does. Because the minute you don't respect what the other person does is the minute you're in trouble.

They might not make as much money as you. They might make substantially more money than you. They might tell you what to do. You might have to tell someone else what to do. It's just this crazy web of people. You have to respect what the other person does to get along. That's one of the things I learned in the small market. If I'm the one sitting there clacking away at the editing deck, you have to respect what they do. Because I know what they go through. I know how hard it is when the machines break and when you have to get stuff done at 5 o'clock and it's 4:58 and it's not done. You pull your hair out.

CASINO PRESIDENT Probably the biggest thing that I've learned is how valuable people are. It doesn't matter how magnificent the building is. It doesn't matter how strong the market is. It's people that really make the business work and make sense. You can have the best strategy in the world and the best building in the world, and if you don't have the hearts and mind of the people who work for you and with you, none of it comes to life.

PR FIRM PARTNER The thing that turns me on is coming up with new ideas, new services, new products. The nice thing is that we have such a great next level of management who can do that day to day business that I can focus on creating a breakthrough product. By trusting management to do their job, it allows me to focus on mine. That's what keeps it fresh for me.

CARDIOVASCULAR TECHNOLOGIST It takes four hands at a scrub table during catherization procedures. Someone manipulates the catheder, somebody injects the coronaries with the contrast. I open them up with guide wires and put in these stints in that open up the arteries. The cardiologist is always manipulating the catheder. We help him by injecting the coronaries and by inflating the ballons to open up the coronaries. There's another one of us in the back room that monitors everything back there. That's pretty much what we do. It's a process where we heavily rely on and trust one another to get the job done.

SUSTAINABILITY ACTIVIST There are some environmentalists that don't have the practical knowledge that a rancher does. Recognize that some ranchers have so much more practical knowledge on how the land works. How do you solve a problem? How do you keep a riverbank from eroding? The ranchers have some really good ideas. We have to get that sense of wisdom from all points of view. Working together to solve problems.

St. Louis, MO

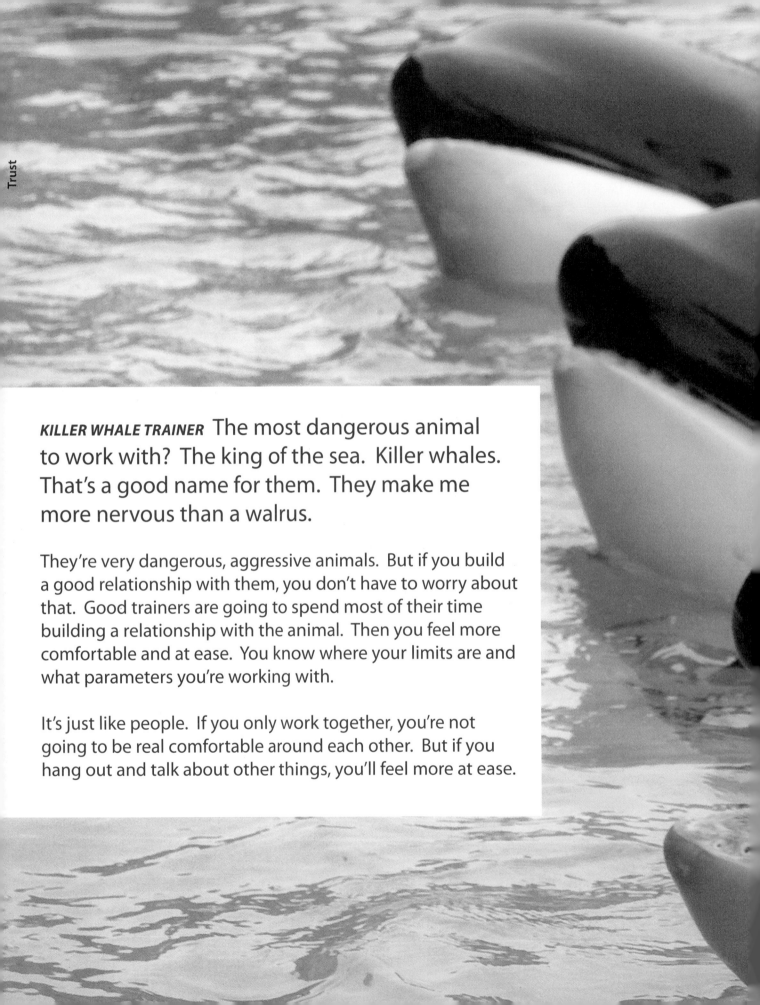

KILLER WHALE TRAINER The most dangerous animal to work with? The king of the sea. Killer whales. That's a good name for them. They make me more nervous than a walrus.

They're very dangerous, aggressive animals. But if you build a good relationship with them, you don't have to worry about that. Good trainers are going to spend most of their time building a relationship with the animal. Then you feel more comfortable and at ease. You know where your limits are and what parameters you're working with.

It's just like people. If you only work together, you're not going to be real comfortable around each other. But if you hang out and talk about other things, you'll feel more at ease.

San Diego, CA

Trust

REGISTERED NURSE What was a surprising thing for me and might have been disappointing was the fact that you can't be as independently thinking as you might want to be. Because you're under a doctor's orders. You may see a situation when you know exactly what to do, but you can't do it until you get an order. I remember feeling frustrated with that as a younger nurse, thinking I know what my patient needs, but I have to get the order. Not being able to be as autonomous was frustrating.

BRAZEN CAREERIST I don't believe that there's one soul mate for every person, and I don't believe that with a job either. I think what we all want is a job that we can control the work. Where we can meet goals. Where we can grow personally. These are not complicated things to have.

BANJO PLAYER A big incentive for me was being in control of something that I thought was going to go somewhere.

REAL ESTATE DEVELOPER Your destiny is in your own hands. That was really important to me.

VIDEO GAME DESIGNER The thing that I like the most about this job is that I can be me. I'm wearing my slippers right now. I'm wearing my ball cap. I'm allowed to be a nerd. I'm allowed to be creative. I'm allowed to not be good at things. Like spreadsheets make me want to vomit. So they have production managers that take care of the spreadsheets. It allows me to specialize in what I like to do and what my strengths are. That's it. I really look forward to coming to work every day.

Yellowstone Park, WY

POUND CAKE PRODUCER The ability that I have to set my own course, to work with great people who have the spirit of this company in mind, that's worth it's weight in gold. I wouldn't trade it for anything.

WRITER I have a rule. The editor, who is my internal critic, can't ever come into the room until after 1 o'clock in the afternoon. If you're a writer, try that. Because the editor tells you how crappy it is. It's a distraction when you can't believe you just wrote the last sentence. But if you just turn off the screen to the computer and make it black, you'll have good sentences if you read your writing. You have to banish the critic. You have to get that critic out of there or you'll never get it on the page. Plus, you rewrite it eight times. Or ten times. You have to trust yourself and say, 'I know what I'm doing.'

HR MANAGER It's funny. Most things that are very successful are not real complicated. If you just try and put yourself in someone else's shoes, it usually works. Because you'll see it, you'll know what they want. And you can give it to them.

CEO We look at everybody as equals and say, 'Here's the stage. How would you perform better than anybody else?'

HR MANAGER People like to come to work at a place where there's a lot of respect and fairness. In most companies, the pay is about equal. The benefits are about equal. But the treatment is all over the place. If you can provide a work environment where people have fun, feel as though they can get ahead, feel that there's a lot of respect, fair treatment and trust, I think they'll stay with you.

Maybe it's the golden rule: Treat people they way they want to be treated. By putting ourselves in their shoes, understanding what they like, what they want, what they need, people respond very positively.

In this game, if you're right three out of five times, you're successful. If you're right two out five times, you're not successful.

It's a very fine line.

We couldn't run our team like the New York Yankees. We couldn't run it like most of the other clubs. Which gives you an opportunity because it gives you an artistic license to do whatever you want, to some extent.

Roll the Credits: P195

Measurability

People want to see themselves progress.

At any given point, people need to know where they stand in their work and how much further they are from their goal.

It's similar to a road trip. When you're traveling, you have road signs giving you estimates of how many miles you have to go before you reach your destination. Sometimes when you've lost hope, those road signs will come along and give you newfound inspiration to continue on in the journey.

Pringle
Custer

Wyoming

In our first keynote speech we did about Pursue the Passion, we closed the speech by sharing the goal of the project. Here's what I said:

"In 5 years, we want to say that we've effectively impacted 1 million Americans and their outlook on work. We want to say that we've impacted 10 million Americans in the next 10 years. And when we die in a fiery RV accident, we want the *New York Times* to write a big fat obituary saying that those 'Pursue the Passion guys' changed the American attitude towards work."

There's a few ways that we are able to measure our work against our goal. We currently have about 1,500 students doing Pursue the Passion interviews as part of the school curriculum. We've done over 100 speeches about our project to audiences ranging from CEO's to 5th graders. We've attracted hundreds of thousands of hits to our website www.pursuethepassion.com. We've done over 300 interviews, traveled over 40,000 miles, been to 40 of the 50 states, and love the random emails and phone calls we receive from people who were inspired by the project.

All of these numbers are tangible measurements showing our impact. Each increase in these numbers gives us fuel in our own tanks to give us a little more mileage than six miles a gallon.

Some people like to be told that they're doing a good job. Other people just want to be left alone to do their work. Regardless of which group you find yourself in, everyone needs an aspect of measurability to their work to let them know whether they are a success. Those measurable aspects of work allow us to gauge our progress and continue on.

BASEBALL GM In this game, if you're right three out of five times, you're successful. Also, if you're right two out of five times, you're not successful. It's a very fine line.

SCREENWRITER Mr. Rogers defined success as 'The love of children and the approbation of your peers.'

PHARMACIST Our job is to get everything right 100% of the time. That's pressure. If you get it wrong, it could cost a patient their life. However, it is a motivator to get everything right.

KILLER WHALE TRAINER Our killer whale show was recognized as the best in the world last year by an outside organization. That makes you feel good about what you do.

AUTHOR This woman writes in and says, 'I read your book. I went into work and I got a raise.' To me, that's the goal. That's when I think it helps to define what success means to you. Not what it's supposed to mean in the context of whatever you're doing.

RADIO JOURNALIST I want to make sure that a story stands on its own journalistically. That it answers the questions that it's trying to raise. And also that it's accurate.

FOOTWEAR DESIGNER This is my NBA. When I turn on the TV, I can see the stuff that I've created on television. That's a big high and an achievement as far as I'm concerned.

ANIMATOR After I did Little Mermaid, moms would walk up to me with their five year old kids. They'd have their little Ariel T-shirts and tell me their daughter loved the movie and that Scuttle was their favorite character. That was all cool.

MARKETING COORDINATOR You plan this whole worldwide tour. You pick the models, buy all the wardrobes, and see if the weather is going to cooperate. And then you see the catalogue. The pictures look awesome and everyone loves them. That's super cool. Seeing the end result is the most rewarding part about the job.

NAME TAG GUY Every once in awhile, someone reaches out to you to let you know that their life has changed because of something you did. It's so insane you can't even believe it. You need to step back and say, 'Wow. This is why I'm doing this.'

The example I have is an email I received from this lady named Katie. She said, 'Scott, I just wanted to say that I really appreciate your philosophy. I'm sixty years old and I have a lot of trouble moving my bowels. Thanks to your blog, I'm now regular every day.' That's the greatest thing that ever happened to me.

If I can make a 60 year old lady regular in her bowel movements because of what I'm doing, then this must be the greatest.

ENTREPRENEURSHIP EXPERT Success isn't just money. Certainly it's about money. I want to make money just like everyone else. But if we never get to that pot of gold, it can't only be about money. We have to figure out what success means to us. Not what our parents told us. Let's figure out what success means for ourselves.

What's success to you?

It's a really good question. I think success is being able to earn a living by doing what you really enjoy. To me, that's success.

Success is being able to feed your children. Success is being able to live in a place that you're comfortable. Success is being able to constantly learn from people that you meet every single day. Success is finding your place in this world where you feel that you can make a contribution. If you can find where you fit in this world, what your contribution is, I think that's really what success is.

EXECUTIVE CHEF The instant feedback from customers is what's best for me. It's not like I sell you a car and six months later you're not happy with it. You either like your meal or you don't. It's immediate gratification. I love that. I think instant gratification is part of every chef's soul.

YOUTH PROGRAM DIRECTOR I have one kid who is going to be a third grader now. He comes from a very rough family. Definitely a lot of gang participation in his family. Not a lot of academic participation in helping their kids out in terms of being successful. He's a problem kid at school.

His teacher wanted to come see him play. She came out one day and watched him, and he worked his tail off. The teacher was like, 'Oh my gosh. I have never seen him work or put that kind of effort forth in anything. It's amazing.'

This opportunity gives him that chance to put effort into something to be successful. Because he doesn't put that effort in at the classroom. He probably doesn't put that effort into anything in his life except this aspect. Ultimately we want to show him that putting effort into anything is the way to achieve success. Whether it's soccer, school, or working at a job.

The impact we have with these kids lives is where it's at. If you get out there and see what effect it has on these kids it makes you want to work that much harder.

LAWYER You take anywhere from six to twelve people who you never met and try to convince them that your clients position is more true than the other side. You don't know these people in the jury box. You don't know what prejudices or what backgrounds they bring. I enjoy the challenge of trying to convince people that I'm more right than the other person.

TEACHER The same way as you would be rewarded by winning like the grandest case ever at being a lawyer, that's when I get a kid who goes from a C to a B. That could be the same level of enjoyment for me. It doesn't have to come with a big paycheck or notoriety or whatever.

THAT GUY I enjoy making quick decisions and getting instant reactions. With the web and technology, the testing is instant. I'll put out something, and within seconds I'll know if it works or not.

If I wanted to open a restaurant, I'd produce a menu and wait three weeks, and still not be sure whether the menu works or not. There's a lot of variables there. That's why the future for me is doing small web companies. Because I can see if what I'm doing is working.

New Orleans, LA

167

MOTIVATIONAL SPEAKER When I was in elementary school I had a terrible time with math and reading. I was not doing well. At that time I wore a hearing aid that was strapped around my chest and ran up to my ears.

I looked like I just stepped off a spaceship.

At that time I had buck teeth, and my teeth were yellow. On the outside I was very happy go lucky, but on the inside I had very low self esteem. They almost held me back in fourth grade. But the powers that be passed me forward. I was put in Mrs. Jordan's fifth grade class.

One day Mrs. Jordan had a question, and I remember knowing that I had the answer. I raised my hand hoping that she wouldn't call on me. Have you ever been in that situation? 'Please don't call on me.' But she did. When she called on me, I answered and she did the most powerful thing.

She said, 'THAT'S RIGHT STEPHEN!'

I sat a little taller in my chair that day. Every one was looking at me. I felt like a Chinese czar.

That's right Stephen. Those three words were like a seed. She planted a seed in my mind. It gave me more confidence than you would ever imagine. When she said those three words, I remember thinking that I was going to make something of myself. I didn't know what, because I was only in fifth grade. But when she said those words, it lit a fire under me.

Today, the ripple effect keeps going. Because I'm still talking about it. I'm telling people that they can make a difference like her. Because my fifth grade teacher said three words.

HR MANAGER

How many people say thanks for being here today?

As opposed to 'You're supposed to be here today. If you weren't here today, I'd write you up.' Because most people come to work every day of their lives. And do we ever thank them?

I don't think companies pay enough attention to it. If they did, more people would be happy with where they work.

Howe, IN

STAGE MANAGER If I go into a job with the idea that the only reason for that job is to step up the ladder, to move up the ladder, then I'm not going to be successful. Because I'm going to step on people. I might be materially successful, and financially successful, but I think for me, stage managing and what I do is a service position. I'm here to service the show and service the actors in a sense of what they need to support them. To listen to them and support the crew and the designers. My only job is to help them.

The way I measure whether I'm successful is if the show is a success.

AUTHOR As a writer, it ends for you when it begins for everyone else. The minute your article is published, you're out there. You're done and you're on your next article. Sometimes you don't hear from people.

If part of your success is that you can know that a million people are reading it, you then wonder if anyone read it. Then you wonder, 'Well, did it make a difference to them?' Or did they just say, 'Oh that's interesting.' And was that enough? Once you get to one level, you start asking yourself these other questions. 'Well, what if it's not a best seller?' That shouldn't be your goal.

You want a book that you can go to bed with at night and feel great about it.

Whatever happens, if it gets panned, you just say that it was what you wanted it to be. I'm not looking for this outside validation. I can sleep at night knowing I did a great job.

SCREENWRITER I could care less about producing box office hits. I don't know how to appeal to a mass audience. It happens or it doesn't. The only thing I can do is please myself. I've found that through pleasing myself, the opinions of people who matter to me have responded positively.

CIRCUS LADY Circus is not about scoring, like a lot of competitive sports. It's about you doing your very best and doing the trick as well and as safely as possible. The whole point is to perform it and share it with the audience. If you do that well, then you're successful.

STREET ARTIST All I do is paint pictures. I don't have another job. I pay my rent, and I pay my car payment. That's enough.

VIDEO GAME DESIGNER On top of finding something that will make you happy, you have to find the comfort of living that you want to be in. On a day to day basis, I have food on the table, bills are paid, and I have enough money for my X Boxes, HD TV's, and that kind of thing. That's all I care about. Everything is covered, and I'm okay with that for now.

PAINTER I didn't realize people were familiar with my work until '99. Once I had a web presence, people started hitting me up, telling me that my paintings meant a lot to them. I never even knew people cared. Maybe I thought people just liked my work because it went well with a couch. Which people still do. But I never realized the impact of my work until I had a web presence and people were able to get at me.

BANJO PLAYER You don't have a resume in this world. Credentials are important, but ultimately, you're judged by the way that you play.

You stand alone that way. And that's weird man, coming from a place like Dartmouth where everyone is saying you have to get your undergrad degree so you can have this piece of paper waiting in the wings to fall back on. It's kind of a façade. My diploma has never done anything for me.

AUTHOR I was at Forbes for five years. When I told my dad that I was leaving he said, 'You know, you're not going to be famous anymore.' First of all, I wasn't famous. But I understood what he meant because there was that brand association just like you would have with Microsoft.

Those brand associations are only successful to a degree. Let's be honest. There's a validity that goes with those types of things. There's a validation that you're good enough to be there. But they only make you happy to a degree. I think you really have to ask yourself what success means to you.

You have to think about that definition.

BASEBALL STATISTICIAN I think setting a good, somewhat reachable goal keeps you motivated and keeps you moving forward. To have those goals just to keep you motivated is good because you never know what you're going to do.

I had no idea setting a goal of getting a PhD was going to get me into baseball. I had no clue. When I set that goal I thought I was going to become an academic. A tenured facility member. But setting that goal got me here.

SKIN CREATOR It's really hard to say when our product is going to be approved and put on the market. It's going to be awhile. Years I'd say. There's definitely been times where it's been a little discouraging, but even though sometimes it's slow, I feel like we're always moving forward and always making some progress.

The reason for that is that we've gotten a really good response from hospitals and the people who would actually be purchasing the product. We just have been getting really good responses from people and we've received a lot of grant money. Those are good measures that we're going in the right direction.

San Francisco, CA

SOCIAL ACTIVIST This morning in the shower I was thinking about being a little more concrete with winnable goals. Although I'd like to see the church go through a reformation, it probably won't happen in this lifetime. It will probably happen through small steps.

PHYSICAL THERAPIST Every patient that I see, whether it be their first visit or their fourth visit, something has changed between those visits. It's a constant changing puzzle that I get to work on every day. Sometimes we don't see progress or there's a lack of progress. Any particular one circumstance is going to require a little bit thought process to figure out how to best benefit this person today.

WRITER Writing isn't the easiest thing to learn. I said that I was going to write 2500 words every day and not leave my desk until I did. It was hard. Some days I could barely get to three hundred words. But I couldn't leave because I set a goal for myself.

SOFTWARE ENGINEER The most difficult part about my job is that it's never done. Like with any product, you can spend a countless amount of time on it and there will always be some configuration or scenario that it breaks. At some point, you have to decide what quality customers are going to use. It would be an appropriate level where we feel comfortable shipping it, even though you know that things may not work. You have to make money, and you have to sell a product. It's just finding that area of where the bar is of what has to be fixed, what needs to be fixed so you can move on to the next release.

INTERNET ENTREPRENEUR I run a internet start-up. I have a site that's about to break 20,000 members and our traffic is in the half million visitors a month. So it's really starting to ramp up.

The site itself makes money with advertising income and sponsorships. It's not enough to survive on. But it's a long term goal. It's pushing through and making it so that hopefully this company survives and makes me enough to live on.

Last November, it was like 4,000 members. In seven or eight months, maybe a year, almost, we doubled traffic twice. I can show you the graph. It's nice to see that. It's exciting. The hard part is that we're not making a lot of money yet. So server costs grow every month. Growing staff. The money isn't there yet, so it's a little bit of a gamble to hope things turn out the way you want them to.

PR FIRM PARTNER Within the first year of opening our business we did a $1 million in billings. End of the second year we had $2.5. Then we went to $5, $7.5, then $9. Then we hit the dot com crash and 9/11. We had a lot of tough years. Now we're back up to $12 million this year with London, San Francisco, Chicago offices in addition to the one here in New York.

ART DIRECTOR It's the end of our fiscal year, so it's a high pressure time. Just nuts. Our fundraising comes in at a very short time period. This year, even shorter and harder because of the economic situation. So I'm looking at our year end projections four times a day. I'm on the phone all day trying to close deals and confirm pledges.

Today, we got an unexpected letter in the mail that was a $10,000 gift from a foundation that we had not applied to and knew nothing about. The gift was in honor of one of our tour guides and their parents in recognition of how important the tour guides are to the museum. That was such a payback.

To me that shows that we're building a family of the museum and everybody is contributing to what that is. It just felt great. We were all standing around reading this letter and virtually in tears because it was so special.

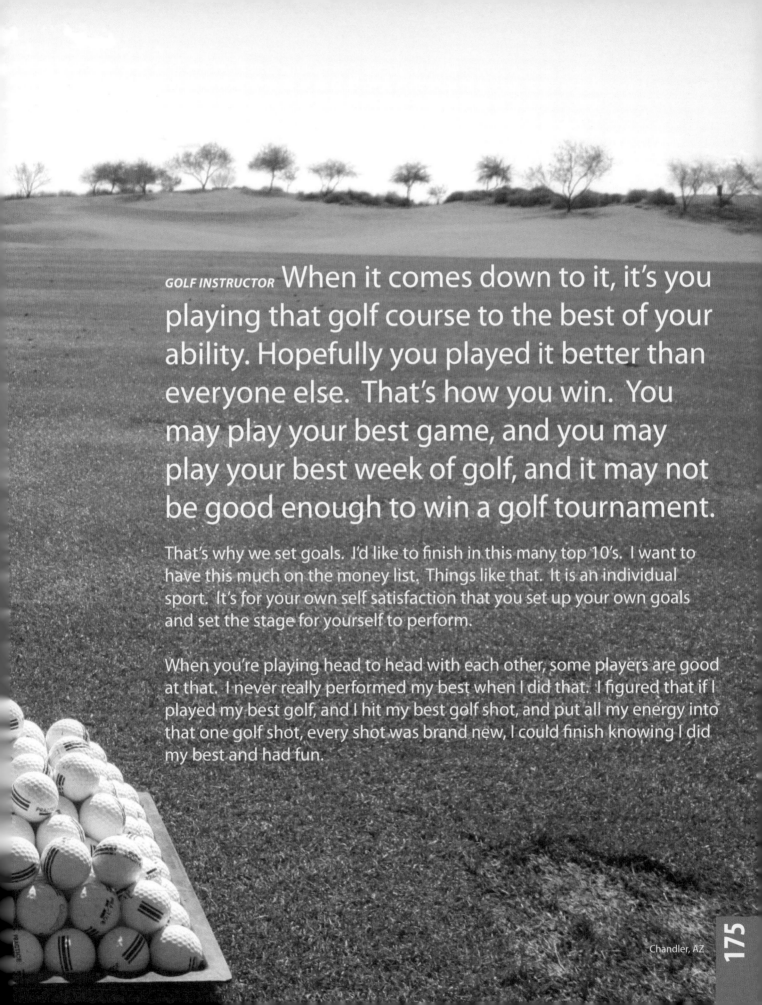

GOLF INSTRUCTOR When it comes down to it, it's you playing that golf course to the best of your ability. Hopefully you played it better than everyone else. That's how you win. You may play your best game, and you may play your best week of golf, and it may not be good enough to win a golf tournament.

That's why we set goals. I'd like to finish in this many top 10's. I want to have this much on the money list. Things like that. It is an individual sport. It's for your own self satisfaction that you set up your own goals and set the stage for yourself to perform.

When you're playing head to head with each other, some players are good at that. I never really performed my best when I did that. I figured that if I played my best golf, and I hit my best golf shot, and put all my energy into that one golf shot, every shot was brand new, I could finish knowing I did my best and had fun.

DOCTOR I've told my kids this many times:

The secret to happiness is find something that you love to do and become the best at it.

Which is the best you can be. Not everyone can be the best in the world. But the best you can be. Then, find someone that will pay you well for it.

That's what it boils down to. Pay you well is according to whatever your goals are. For me it's to be able to raise my family and do things that are meaningful to me. For others it may be to make millions of dollars. My hat's off to them. Whatever it means.

Put A & B together.

Washington D.C.

REAL ESTATE INVESTOR You just have to look forward and drive on and succeed according to whatever success means to you. For me it means being excellent at what you do. Being in the top 5 at something. If you're a company in the XYZ industry you're a top 5 company or you're in the top 5%. That, for me, is success.

PHOTOGRAPHER I have the most published photographs that have appeared in the magazine. More of my shots have made the cover than any other Playboy photographer in history. I've photographed Pamela Anderson and just about every other major name you can think of. So yes, I've been fortunate enough to achieve a high degree of success.

BASEBALL EXECUTIVE The biggest accomplishment was figuring out a way to get a privately financed ballpark built. In the face of a lot of the finance experts. I'm not a finance guy but a lot of the smart finance experts said there was no way we could ever do it. And we did it. We did a lot of things right. We got lucky on a couple things. But actually getting the ballpark built after all those years…four failed elections… team almost moving again…that's obviously the biggest accomplishment. It was like our version of climbing Mount Everest.

RESTAURANT MANAGER We've never repeated a dish here in 19 years. Once a dish is off the menu, it's gone. It's done. It's finished. It's the past. We make 30-40 different plates a month. The menu is always changing. Over 19 years, with 30 different plates a month, you do the math to figure out how many we've done. And we've never repeated one.

We have one client here who is a banker from New York. He lived here in Chicago for seven or eight years. He's dined with us over 350 times. He's never had the same dish twice.

Those are the challenges we love. People come to this restaurant thinking that they don't want what they've had before. We love to meet these expectations.

SALARY ARBITRATOR The challenge of working here is that failure is not an option. Mistakes don't happen. If you make mistakes, you're out of a job. Because this department is very high profile in that we are constantly on the phone with club people. We are constantly sending out memorandums. Always issuing advice. You can't be wrong. Being wrong one time might cost a club hundreds of thousands of dollars, or even a player. Being wrong is not an option.

The insistence on perfection is a challenge, but a great challenge.

ACCOUNT EXECUTIVE I'm going to make the calls. I'm going to sell the tickets. I'm going to hit the goals. Whatever the challenge is, you throw down and you know where you stand.

That's the one thing in sales. There's always a number to gauge you by. Here's my number and here's Joe Blow's number. Who did better? It's not that hard to figure out.

SALES DIRECTOR We sold 32,000 tickets and brought in an extra $500,000 with our special events program. So it got the attention of the organization.

HOTEL OWNER Success and failure really is measured by the bottom line. No ifs, ands, ors, buts about it.

ROCKET SCIENTIST The cool thing about rockets is that it's a definite, 'It worked!' Or 'It didn't work.' If it works, it feels good.

FILM COMMISSIONER Our commission is responsible for an annual economic impact of $90 million as a result of the film projects we attract to San Diego. That's a huge motivating factor in what we do.

TASTEMASTER The goal is to create a final product that R&D likes, the National Advisory Board likes, the franchises like, and customers like. That is where you want to be. Then it's ready to go nationwide. And that's the ultimate goal.

POSTER SHOP MANAGER People who have never seen this shop before come in and say, 'I've never seen anything like this!' I still get it after 23 years of working here. That makes me feel good about having the passion to operate this shop.

CONSERVATIONIST What we've done the last twenty years is spreading the gloom and doom of the world. 'We're polluting the water! We're polluting the air! Animals are becoming endangered! Everything we're doing to the planet is wrong!'

What I do is I travel and look for successes and share that progress with people. When I go to the rain forest, I see a patch that was slashed and burned that is coming back again. I go to Alaska and I see brown bears populations that are really good. I see eagle populations. Years ago I went to Los Angeles and saw 70 gray whales. Now there's over 700 down there. The alligator came off back the endangered species list in '85. There's all these stories you never hear about that show we are progressing!

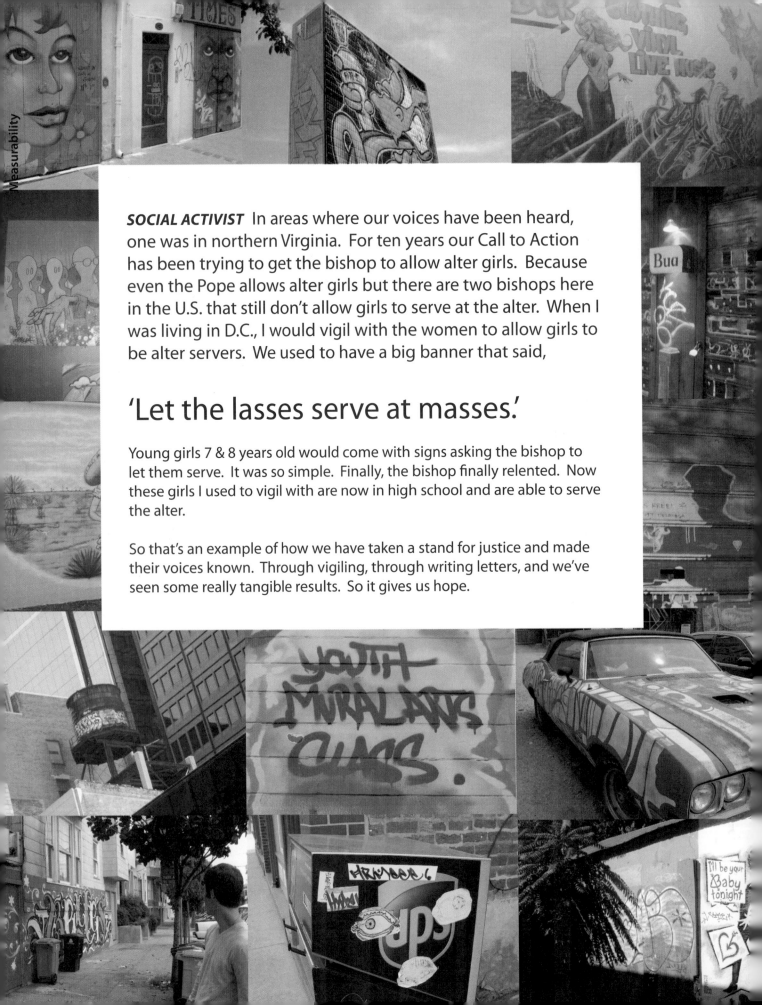

SOCIAL ACTIVIST In areas where our voices have been heard, one was in northern Virginia. For ten years our Call to Action has been trying to get the bishop to allow alter girls. Because even the Pope allows alter girls but there are two bishops here in the U.S. that still don't allow girls to serve at the alter. When I was living in D.C., I would vigil with the women to allow girls to be alter servers. We used to have a big banner that said,

'Let the lasses serve at masses.'

Young girls 7 & 8 years old would come with signs asking the bishop to let them serve. It was so simple. Finally, the bishop finally relented. Now these girls I used to vigil with are now in high school and are able to serve the alter.

So that's an example of how we have taken a stand for justice and made their voices known. Through vigiling, through writing letters, and we've seen some really tangible results. So it gives us hope.

RELOCATION DIRECTOR We're responsible of the movement of 25,000 families through the ten year period. We're in year seven right now. We're going to finish the plan. Our CEO is dead set on finishing.

I feel that we will finish. If I didn't feel like it, I wouldn't stay here.

CEO At our company we have 9,200 employees. One of the greatest accomplishments a leader can have is to be able to influence a group of people to go towards a commitment of quality and financial performance. If you're able to share a vision and see that people are pursuing that vision, I think that is the highest of your accomplishments.

MOTIVATIONAL SPEAKER I like to visualize. When you look at my refrigerator, I have a picture of Oprah. It's my dream to be on her talk show. I also have a cut out of the *New York Times* best seller list. I put my name on top of it. It's my dream to have a best selling book. And I have a picture of a plane that I would like to fly. It's all on my refrigerator.

I see it every single day. It keeps me going. That's what helps.

SOFTWARE ENGINEER You gain confidence by doing something and succeeding. For example, if you look at my white board right now, these are things I'm working on. As they get done, I go through and I check them off. That builds confidence. Right now I'm only about a third of the way done, but as I get to the middle, that builds confidence. As you build confidence in areas, your influence grows in scope.

How many times do we actually finish what we start?

If you can remain focused on that cradle to grave kind of credo, incorporate components of measurability to know where you stand, you'll eventually cross the goal line.

Are we there yet?

College grads traveling across the country
to meet passionate professionals who their jobs

Pursue The Passion

www.pursuethepassion.com

2007

www.pursuethepassion.com

Pursue The Passion

Find Out More
www.pursuethepassion.com

West Yellowstone, WY

Pursue The Passion

How does this all come together?

We've identified the three elements of a pursuit with Ownership, Risk, and Hard Work. We've identified where the passion comes from with Significance, Trust, and Measurability. How do you combine all these puzzle pieces to get a complete picture?

What we found is that if employers provide people with the three things they need in work: Significance, Trust, Measurability, then it leads to those fundamental behaviors of Ownership, Risk, and Hard Work.

If employers give their employees significance, if they share the vision with them and make work relevant, employees will want to take ownership. They'll want to take a hold of their career and dictate where it will go.

If employers and managers trust employees to do the job they were hired to do, employees become much more entrepreneurial and take risks to solve problems and create solutions. When there's an organization full of risk taking people who are willing to go all in, that's an organization that will do some great things.

If employees are able to measure how their work is making a difference, then people will set higher goals and work harder to achieve those goals.

When all of these things come together, it equates to passion in work.

Significance

Ownership

Trust

Risk

Measurability

Hard Work

To close out every interview, we asked our interviewees the question, 'If you could go back to when you were 22 years old, and offer yourself just one piece of advice, what would you tell your 22 year old self?'

If I were to offer myself a piece of advice when I was a confused college grad debating what to do on the journey ahead, I'd offer three words: Pursue the Passion.

If I were to offer that up to my 22 year old self, the younger me would probably have no idea what the older me was talking about. But that's okay. The answers aren't always clear. As long as those three words stuck with me when crucial decisions had to be made, a lot of big question marks (like 'What should I do with my life?') would be much easier to answer.

Because what happens is that those three words turn into a compass that guides you on the journey. When teachers and peers say that you're not cut out for a certain thing, the words 'pursue the passion' can help you prove the doubters wrong. When self doubt creeps in and you don't believe in yourself, the words 'pursue the passion' reassure you that you're on the right track. When obstacles, excuses, and environmental shifts stand in the way of doing what you really want to do, the words 'pursue the passion' can be the fuel to help you push through the barriers.

So if there's one thing that I'd want you to takeaway from this book, here's the cliff notes that can serve as the roadmap for your own journey:

Pursue the Passion.

Roll the Credits

ACCOUNT EXECUTIVE My name is Cory Shakarian. I do business in sports sales. Sports is an emotional roller coaster of a business. When you're selling in sports, whether the team wins or loses determines how you do the next day at work. My best times are always when we're winning.

Los Angeles, CA

ACCOUNTANT My name is Mary Gilbaugh. I'm the Controller for the Phoenix Suns. I said when I was ten that I wanted to work in professional sports and finance. I'm twenty-six and I'm here, so I couldn't be any happier at this point.

ACCOUNTING PROFESSOR My name is Katie Cordova. I'm an accounting lecturer at the Eller College Management at the University of Arizona.

Phoenix, AZ

ANIMATOR My name is Rick Farmiloe. People say to me, 'You're so lucky. You don't have to work for a living. You just draw! You don't have a regular job.' It is a job, but I like it. That's the difference. It is a lot of work. It's just that I enjoy it.

ART DIRECTOR I'm Susan Krane. I'm the director of the Scottsdale Museum of Contemporary Art. The director does tons of stuff at the same time in as short a time as possible. Mainly, making the museum go and grow.

Burbank, C

ASSISTANT GM My name is Fred Ulhman Jr. I knew I wanted to be in baseball since I was five years old. Now here I am. I've been the assistant general manager of the San Diego Padres baseball club for ten years.

ASSOCIATE PRODUCER My name is Dave Knudsen. I'm an associate producer at the video game production company, Rainbow Studios in Phoenix. My job is to make sure that certain deadlines are met and we stay within budget. I clear the way so people can work.

ASSOCIATE SOFTWARE ENGINEER My name is Andrew Hair. I originally wanted to be a video game designer. But I found out through that internship experience that I enjoyed computer programming a lot better. So that's what I do for Rainbow Studios.

San Diego, C

ASSOCIATE TV PRODUCER I'm Holly. I'm an associate producer for Northwest Afternoon which is the longest running talk show in the nation. It's a great job. I mean, I had baby tigers on the show the other day. I got to meet Mario Lopez. It's great. The job really fills my life up with inspiration.

ASTROLOGER My name is Laurence Hillman. Astrologers have always looked at whether the time is right. That's our job. It's foretelling certain logics. It's the same way that a weatherman says there is a storm coming from this direction. Astrology is the same thing.

San Diego,

AUDIO VIDEO DESIGNER My name is Donna Fabbri. I love sound. I love visuals. I love what it does from engineering and marketing. I can listen to any kind of music. If I'm awake, music has to be on.

Seattle, WA

AUTHOR My name is Joanne Gordon. I love writing. I love the puzzle part of it. I often describe writing as putting together a puzzle, but someone threw away the top of the box. At the end of it, it looks like a picture that's always been there. But when you first get it, it's just pieces everywhere. And you have to figure out what the picture is.

BACKFIELD EDITOR My name is Keith Leighty. I'm a backfield editor for the New York Tiems. Reporters write the stories and from there they come to my desk. I make sure the article is solid and sound in its reporting.

BANJO PLAYER My name is Chris Pandolfi. I play the banjo in the bluegrass group, the Infamous Stringdusters.

San Francisco, CA

BASEBALL EXECUTIVE I'm Pat Gallagher. I'm the President of San Francisco Giants Enterprises. This is my thirtieth year with the team. I certainly didn't set out to be in one place for thirty years. But I'm going to keep doing it as long as it's fun.

BASEBALL GM My name is Billy Beane. I'm the General Manager for the Oakland A's. I love the game. When I was a kid I played my own sudo fantasy games. Building a team was always ultimately what I wanted to do, career wise. I love playing a fantasy rotisserie baseball. Somehow I'm able to get paid to do it.

Phoenix, AZ

BASEBALL STATISTICIAN My name is Jim Cassandro. I'm in baseball operations. Which means that I contribute information to the Diamondbacks from the statistical end of things in terms of player evaluations.

BASKETBALL COACH My name is Lute Olson. I recently retired from coaching at the University of Arizona. I've never felt like I've gone to work in fifty years. Other than the summers when I drove gas transports for Texaco in Southern California.

Tucson, AZ

BASKETBALL EXECUTIVE My name is Rick Welts. I'm the President of the Phoenix Suns. I also came up with the idea for All Star Weekend, the Dream Team marketing slogan for USA Basketball, and helped create the WBNA. I'm one of the luckiest people in the world.

BASKETBALL PLAYER My name is Antoine Broxi. I've played ball in places like Bangladesh, Venezuela, Czech Republic, Qatar, Dubai, China, Saudi Arabia. What makes it worth it? Just listen to that sound behind us. That's a great feeling.

Phoenix, AZ

BATTALION CHIEF My name is Lisa Clinchy. We're running into burning buildings when everyone else is running out. That's what we do as firefighters. So calling us heroes for doing what we love to do just doesn't seem to make sense to us. We do it every day. That's what we love to do.

BAR OWNER My name is Arman Ausiello. I own Ausiello's Fifth Street Bar and Grill in Santa Rosa, California. Some people might call us a sports bar. To me, we're a neighborhood tavern that's very sports oriented that puts out a good, consistent product. That's how we survive.

BARTENDER My name is Zack Verden. I'm temporarily bartending in Seattle, Washington while I get things together.

BEER BREWER My name is Charles Finkle. I love my job because I'm associated with a product that gives great pleasure to the people. And that's beer.

BLOGGER My name is Eric Boheme, and my website is known as the Blogging Boss. I started to blog primarily because being in business, and being in Corporate America for almost eighteen, twenty years or whatever, people need to hear the voice of reason.

BOOK STORE MANAGER My name is Cindy Dach. Every couple of years I look back and I'm still surprised at where I ended up. Like General Manager of a bookstore? I kicked and screamed that I never would be doing that. But it's like every year you get smarter and you learn things and you face a new challenge. It's a good fit.

BOXER Name's Anthony 'The Bullet' Bosante. Got a fight this Friday. Gonna bust somebody up.

BOXING GYM OWNER My name is Lisa Bauch. I'm 43. I'm the only woman to solely own and operate a boxing gym in America.

BOXING TRAINER My name is Bill Kaehn. I'm from Minneapolis. I was born into the fight game. I've been in boxing sixty-six years. I love the game. When that bell rings you crawl up those steps. There's nobody there except for you and God Almighty. And the guy in front of you that is going to take your head off if he can do it.

BRAZEN CAREERIST My name is Penelope Trunk. I think people respect the idea that you should love what you do. It's actually a radical idea. To love what you do. That's why we don't have career paths. You're blazing a non traditional career path.

BROWNIE PRODUCER My name is David Kravetz. I co-founded Fairytale Brownies. I really think it's great to sell brownies. Of all the things in the world I could be selling…it's a fun product, it brings smiles to people's faces, and people love chocolate.

Phoenix, AZ

BUS DRIVER My name is Mike from Minneapolis. I'm a bus driver for the Metro Transit. Lots of bus drivers don't realize they are in a customer oriented, service type of business. Some drivers won't let riders short a couple of quarters on the bus. Some don't talk to nobody all day. Just put they head down and drive. Not me man. I'm all about the customer, all about the people. I'm a people person, man.

BUSINESS AUTHOR My name is Jackie Freiberg. I'm the author of BOOM! What I do is aim to liberate people's thinking, challenge them to change, and show them how to do it.

San Diego, CA

CAMERAMAN My name is Doug Irvine. I'm a freelance cameraman in Seattle. I move electrons, listen to sound…very cerebral sort of things.

CAR SALESMAN My name is Jim Click. I'm the owner of the Jim Click Automotive Group. We have numerous auto dealerships and are one of the top groups in the country.

CARDIOVASCULAR TECHNOLOGIST My name is Robbie from Fairfax, Virginia. A lot of people haven't heard of what we do. People come in and they're like, 'What are you guys? Nurses?' There are lots of people with titles and job descriptions that people really don't know much about.

Seattle, WA

CAREER COACH My name is Laura Allen. I'm the founder of 15second pitch.com. What I love to do is help people figure out they really want to do with their lives and help them communicate that in a 15 second pitch.

CAREER COUNSELOR My name is Shelia Curran. I'm the Executive Director of the Duke University Career Center.

Tucson, AZ

CARTOONIST My name is Jason Kotecki, and this is my wife Kim. Together, we're speakers. The core message that we talk is about adultitis. Basically, taking yourself too seriously. I produce a comic strip too that features a skunk. He's the mascot for our company slogan, 'Adulthood stinks.'

CASINO PRESIDENT My name is Renee West. I grew up here in Las Vegas. I needed a job, so might as well work for the industry that represents our state. I'm the President of the Excalibur. I'm the first female executive to manage a property on the strip.

Madison, WI

CELEBRITY CHEF My name is Alex Guarnaschelli. I am the Executive Chef at Butter restaurant on Lafayette Street in Manhattan. I get pissy and disagreeable if I go a few days without making a salad or a soup or something.

CEO My name is Gamal Aziz. I'm the CEO of MGM Mirage in Las Vegas, Nevada. For the last two years, MGM Grand has been named Best Place to Work. Those are the only two awards I put next to me on my desk because that's the thing I'm most proud of.

New York, NY

CHARACTER ARTIST My name is Samuel Howard. A senior character artist takes concept art and brings characters to life in video games. If you can't draw, you can't have my job. I draw all the time.

CHEMICAL ENGINEER My name is Joel Dickinson. I'm an engineer for sustainability initiatives and technologies for the Salt River Project in Arizona. I went back to school when I was 32 years old.

Occidental, CA

CHIEF FINANCIAL OFFICER My name is Deb Morrin. I'm working on bring a luxury health resort to the Chicago area. We're still about two years away from operation, but we know our end goal and are working towards it each day.

CHIEF OF INFRASTRUCTURE My name is Joseph Harmening. I am the Chief of Infrastructure for the Mayor's Office of the City of Chicago. Infrastructure reaches into every corner of our lives. I think, 'If I build this road, it's going to make so and so's life much easier.' My job has such an awesome responsibility that it can be a little bit scary at times.

Washington DC

CHIEF OF STAFF My name is Maura Polichelli. I am the chief of staff to Congresswoman Gabrielle Giffords who represents Southern Arizona.

CHILD THERAPIST My name is Oren Matteson. I don't have second thoughts about my career. I couldn't do anything else. I have friends and family in real estate and law and medicine and investment banking and all this stuff. I couldn't imagine doing that for a day. Being around kids and making a difference with them is the only thing I see myself doing.

Santa Monica, CA

CHILDREN'S AUTHOR My name is Christine Peymani. I teach freshman English at USC and have published five books in the Bratz series for younger girls. I'm actively working to produce books that intrigue the next generation of media consumers.

CIRCUS LADY My name is Jessica Hentoff. I've known circus to be my life's path since I was 18. I've been really blessed to be able to share the gift of circus across the globe. Just being like Peter Pan and sprinkling the magic fairy dust on people. It's really magical, and it's why I do it.

Chicago, I

CLOTHING STORE OWNER My name is Dave Martinez. I own a hip hop clothing store in LA and have my own record label. Clothing and music now is a rip off of another piece that has already been done. You either play along or you don't survive.

Redlands, CA

CO-WORKING ATTENDANT My name is Alex Hillman and I'm the founder of Independents Hall, a co-working space in Philly. I run and maintain a space that's like a hybrid between office and a café for independent contractors and freelancers.

COFFEE WHOLESALER My name is Tommy Thwaites and I am the co-founder of Coda Coffee in Denver, Colorado. The other co-founder is my brother Tim. I've been involved with coffee since I was 18, and I'm going on fourteen years now.

Durham, NC

COLLECTOR My name is Mark Conway. No one is going to care about your destiny more than you. You're the architect of it. The best things that have ever happened to me were totally unforeseen and they came about because of my taking risks.

COLLEGE PROFESSOR My name is John W. F. Dulles. I've been a college professor since 1962. I'm a professor of Latin American studies at the University of Texas. I'm 94 years old.

San Francisco, CA

COLLEGE STUDENT My name is Brandon and I'm a sophomore at Duke University. I'm a double major in Chemistry and History. I actually have no idea what I want to do with those majors, but I love them both. That's the way you view things, I've heard. Just be happy.

COMMERCIAL PROPERTY MANAGER My name is Phil Rapoport. I'm the General Manager of the Transamerica Pyramid Center. The building is the tallest and most recognizable skyscraper in the San Francisco skyline.

COMMERCIAL REAL ESTATE AGENT My name is Andrew Ackerman. I'm two months into working for Cushman Wakefield in New York City. I'm excited about the job because I have the potential to make a lot of money. But for now, I'm wearing my dad's Rolex to keep up the appearance.

New York, NY

COMMUNICATIONS DIRECTOR My name is Dave Santucci. I'm the Director of Communications for the world's largest aquarium, the Georgia Aquarium. I always say it's a good day at work when I get to see fish. That's obviously every day.

COMMUNICATIONS DIRECTOR My name is Tim Katzman. Someone asked me a week ago to describe my position. I borrowed a football comparison and said that I'm the editorial free safety for the San Diego Padres. The organization expects and demands that I understand what a misplaced modifier is.

Atlanta, GA

COMMUNITY CENTER ORGANIZER My name is Cindy Banks. Last year I saw a beautiful, retired church and I dreamt of opening it as a community center. The way it stands now I'm still working full-time, I'm deeply in debt and I stand about a 50/50 chance of pulling my dream off. If I'm able to make it work, it's going to be unbelievable.

Portland, OR

CONSERVATIONIST My name is Peter Gros. I'm the co-host of Mutual of Omaha's Wild Kingdom and a public speaker. What I'm passionate about until I die is convincing as many young people as I can that it's not too late to make a difference. We haven't destroyed the planet. We definitely have serious problems. But we're turning the corner.

CROSSWORD PUZZLE CREATOR My name is Jan Buckner Walker. At one point I was a lawyer, but I now create crossword puzzles for my company, Kids Across, Parents Down. The puzzles feature across clues for kids, and down clues for parents. We're nationally syndicated in newspapers and are in restaurants. We're looking to go international right now. There's so many options.

New York, NY

DANCE INSTRUCTOR My name is Marcella Kaye Sullivan. I run an educational program called Dance Across The Curriculum in North Carolina.

DESIGNER My name is Jason Mayden. I'm a designer for the Jordan Brand at Nike. The separation of 'self' and 'product' is very important in my work. No one knows that I designed it, so the product has to hold its own and speak for itself. At the end of the day, its all about your product.

Durham, NC

DISASTER VOLUNTEER My name is Saundra Grayes. I'm a Katrina evacuee. I'm the head cook here with Common Ground. Everyone like my cooking. I can cook anything you ask me to cook. I made a crawfish, egg shrimp and feed last night. Over pork roast and some rice. I can't count how many meals I've done since I've been here. Maybe 10,000 plates?

DOCTOR My name is John Freedman. I have several passions. Medicine is a calling and a passion. I do third world medical work. Travel is a passion. I've been to a little over 80 countries at this point. And my family. We've been able to blend these passions and share some of it all together.

Santa Rosa, CA

DOCUMENTARIAN My name is Brian Conley. I'm the co-founder of a project called Alive In Baghdad. The gimmick or whatever is stories from Iraq from Iraqis. We're taking our privileges as filmmakers and saying that we don't need another story from a white guy in the suburbs. Whether or not you're for or against the war, it's pretty important to hear from the people whom the war is affecting most directly.

Philadelphia, PA

DONATION ADVOCATE My name is Sandra Madera. I do any kind of speaking in Spanish to the community for One Legacy. One Legacy is a transplant donor network that serves Southern California. So I do presentations, volunteer training, things like that.

Chicago, IL

DRUG MANUFACTURER My name is Marc Fages. I manage a commodity. Chemicals and small molecules and their raw materials, meaning that we're going to use them for further processing and they are going to end up in drug products that we give to humans.

EMPOWERMENT OFFICER My name is Robyn Williams. I run the Choice Center, a leadership training center in Las Vegas, Nevada.

ENGINEERING ENTREPRENEUR My name is Irv Segal. I'm a 46-year old entrepreneur who has founded 40 startups before I finally got it right with SysGen Inc.

Chicago, IL

ENTREPRENEURIAL EXPERT My name is Barry Moltz. I have worked for one of the largest companies in the world. I have been fired more than once. I have started three businesses. I sold my last business. Hopefully what I had to say in this book was a little different than all the other crap you read.

ENVIRONMENT ARTIST My name is Leslie Carerra-Keys. I'm a senior environment artist at the video game company, Rainbow Studios. Basically all the environments you see in a video game is what we create. So we come up with the sky, and the all the elements that are captured in the scene. We draw a lot.

Long Beach, CA

EPIDEMIOLOGIST My name is Amanda Latimore. My life does not consist of white lab coats and microscope slides. My background is in the social sciences, and I use that background to gain a better understanding of the habits of marginalized populations. This includes sex workers, the homeless, and those suffering from diseases related to HIV and AIDS.

EVENT PLANNER My name is Faham Zakariaei. I oversee all the special events for the San Francisco Giants. I pick the games where attendance isn't going to be very high and hold special theme nights on them. Singles Night, College Night, Irish Heritage Night…anything you can think of. It's kind of like my dream job because I get to work for a team that I love.

San Francisco, CA

EXECUTIVE CHEF My name is Nicolaas Burr. I'm an executive chef in Atlanta, Georgia. I'm the executive chef at a farmhouse restaurant. That's what I do. We always have a good time.

EXECUTIVE TV PRODUCER I'm the executive producer of Scarborough Country. It's a show of Joe Scarborough, a Congressman that's on every night at 9 o'clock. It's not really a political show, but its politics and pop culture.

New York, NY

FILM COMMISSIONER My name is Cathy Anderson. I'm the President of the San Diego Film Commission. Today, our commission is responsible for an annual economic impact of $90 million as a result of the film projects we attract to San Diego.

Phoenix, AZ

FINANCIAL ANALYST My name is Dan Fumai. I'm the VP of Finance for the San Diego Padres. About twenty five percent of my life is dealing with financial statements and the debt service rule. It's a grind with a lot of spreadsheets.

FINANCIAL PLANNER My name is Andrew Avella. I'm the founder and principal of the Retirement Portfolio Specialists, which assists individuals and business owners in understanding their retirement plan alternatives.

Beaverton, OR

FIRE CAPTAIN My name is Doug Graham. I'm a captain here at fire station 18. I've been a firefighter for 22 years now. I was hooked the first time I visited a firehouse. I went through four years of testing and came on at 25.

FISH MONGER My name is Jim. I smell like fish all the time. I work at the Pike Place Market in Seattle. Want to catch a fish?

FOOTWEAR DESIGNER My name is D'Wayne Edwards. I am the Footwear Design Director for the Jordan Brand at Nike. I use the same type of number two pencil that I used in middle school. That's how I get down. Just a regular old piece of copy room paper and a pencil.

Chicago, IL

FREELANCE WRITER My name is Jacob Gordon. Most of my waking working hours are dedicated to TreeHugger. Get sustainable or die tryin'.

FROZEN CUSTARD RETAILERS My name is Denny and this is my wife Mardi. We're the owners of Scooter's Frozen Custard, a retail shop located on Belmont and Paulina in Chicago. Realtors use Scooter's as a positive selling point for the neighborhood, residents use it as a place to convene, and the kids love the custard. Especially in the summer.

GARDENER My name is Anne Jaeger. I'm amazed to not have a mulch pile right now. I feel kind of naked without one. Everyone needs a mulch pile.

Lake Oswego, OR

GENEALOGIST My name is Leslie Lawson. I help restore a sense of family within families. I bright light to family information that may be buried forever without my services.

GRAPHIC DESIGNER My name is Jason Thompson and I'm the only graphic designer at Prisma Graphic in Phoenix, Arizona. I've always loved computers and I've always loved drawing and designing stuff. It just has worked out for me.

Beaverton, OR

GOAT FARMER My name is Linda Harrison. My husband and I breed goats in Hermitage, Tennessee. People can't believe I remember the name to every goat on our farm. To me, they're just as different as people you know.

Hermitage, TN

GUITAR SCHOOL INSTRUCTOR My name is Dan Emery. I'm the founder of the largest Guitar School in New York City. I've hustled really hard in my life and have achieved a modest level of success that I'm proud of.

HEALTHCARE DIRECTOR My name is Peter Miller. I'm the Director of Vanderbilt Health Tech Laboratories here in Nashville.

HEALTHCARE ENTREPRENEUR My name is Wayne McVicker. I started as an architect, ended up in healthcare, started a software company, took it public. We were the first IPO of 2000, 16th largest gain in history. Rode the boom up and down. Wrote a book about it. Started another software company. Doing it again.

New York, NY

HEDGE FUND MANAGER My name is Whitney Johnson. What I do in my day job is I'm working on a hedge fund with a professor at Harvard Business School and his son.

HELICOPTER PILOT My name is Bruce Haffner. I remember being in first grade and seeing a helicopter land at my school assembly. I now fly News Chopper3 in Phoenix. What could be better than flying around town as the sun sets and rises, going to each reported accident or following a high speed chase? It beats working for a living.

Phoenix, AZ

HIGH SCHOOL PRINCIPAL I'm Chris Jones. I'm the principal of Central High School. Home of the Bobcats. A large 5A high school in Phoenix.

HOSPITALITY PUBLICIST My name is Jennifer Baum. I'm the owner of Bullfrog & Baum, a public relations firm that focuses on hospitality. I have a pretty cool job. But it's not all glamour. It's a lot of hard work.

New York, NY

HOTEL MANAGER My name is Leon Young. I started out in the hotel industry as a graveyard security guard after my son was born. The hotel industry kind of saved my life. It helped me swallow my pride. Being in service roles has helped me grow as an individual. Now I'm 38 and I'm the GM of the brand new W Hotel in Scottsdale.

HOTEL OWNER My name is Greg Bennett. I own the Konocti Harbor Resort. I've created the property as you see it. I built probably 75% of it. I built the Amphitheatre. I created the show room. I book the talent. I produce the talent. I write the radio spots. I'm involved with all that, but without the passion, I don't think I'm here.

St. Louis, MO

HR MANAGER My name is Arte Nathan. I think I was born to do Human Resources. I love this. Every day I come in to this job just full of energy. What can I try today? What can I come up with that will make people say that this is a great place to work?'

Irvine, CA

HUMANITARIAN My name is Helene Gayle. I am the President and CEO of CARE, a leading humanitarian organization fighting global poverty. I've been very fortunate to have incredible opportunities to use my life in a way that is very fulfilling, but also makes a contribution to societies around the world.

INNOVATION DIRECTOR My name is Tobie Hatfield. I'm the innovation director of the Nike Innovation Kitchen in Beaverton, Oregon. The Kitchen is a designers think tank. It's where we cook up the shoes.

Portland, OR

INSURANCE AGENT My name is Joy Estes. For the last 27 years, I've been a State Farm agent. I help individuals, families, and businesses select insurance policies that provide the best protection for their lives, health, and property.

INTERIOR DESIGNER My name is Jen Hankee. I'm an interior designer for a hospitality design firm in Chicago. I've worked on hotel projects in downtown Chicago, Florida, Virginia, and condos in Jamaica.

INTERNET ENTREPRENEUR My name is Darius Monsef IV. I run COLOURlovers, which is a creative color design resource on the web. I want to continue to do the internet start up stuff. I have an overactive creative gland.

San Francisco, CA

INVENTOR My name is Dave Mathews. I've been taking things apart and finding ways to put them back together since I was in kindergarten. It's gotten to the point where I've earned the nickname, 'Gadget Guy.'

IT GUY Terry. I work in QA and work on software in Seattle. My job changes all the time. I'm always doing something different. I'm always working with new technologies.

JANITOR My name is Miguel. My family moved from Mexico to Minneapolis four years ago. I love America, I love my life, and I love my job.

Phoenix, A

JOB BOARD EXECUTIVE My name is Brian Mohr. I'm the Senior Vice President of Jobing.com. It's good work that we do. We help job seekers get jobs and help employers find people. It actually matters to the community.

KILLER WHALE TRAINER My name is Robin Sheets and I run Shamu Stadium at Sea World in San Diego. A lot of my job deals with marine biology, and being a veterinarian, and even oceanography. But really, I'm a behaviorist. I motivate killer whales to do certain things by modifying their behavior through relationships I build

San Diego, C

LAWYER My name is Lonnie Williams Jr. I was the first African American lawyer in Phoenix in a large firm. I'm now a partner at Quarles & Brady.

LEADERSHIP STRATEGIST My name is Steve Farber. I've been working in leadership development for the last twenty years. It's my passion to cultivate leadership at all levels in an organization.

Chicago, IL

LECTURE AGENT My name is Lisa Brandsdorf. I'm the President of the University Division for the Greater Talent Network. My job is to book speakers like Lance Armstrong, Donald Trump, Ben & Jerry and hundreds of others at colleges across the nation.

LEGAL ADVOCATE My name is Evan Casper Futterman. We're the legal advocacy of Common Ground in New Orleans. It's a combination of community organizing and general service provision and immediate, daily needs.

College grads traveling across the country to meet passionate professionals who ... the
Mesa, AZ

LIFE COACH My name is Pam Slim. My work, as I view it in the big picture, is reconnecting people with that essential fire.

LIFE COACH My name is Jesse Gros. There's so much anxiety around what you're going to do. I always try to tell people that it's the tiny little baby steps that make a difference.

MAGAZINE EDITOR My name is Anita Malik. I'm Asian-American so I thought that there needed to be a magazine for this market. I researched and there was nothing. So now I'm the founder and editor of East West.

Cary, IL

OUTPLACEMENT MANAGER I'm Mindy Rackison from Northridden, a town outside of Boston. I've fired a lot of people. Hundreds of them. It doesn't get any easier to do it.

MASSEUSE My name is JoAnne Pavin. My passion is helping others live a healthy, balanced lifestyle. In addition to massage services, I help people live more energetic lives through seminars and healthy products.

MARKETING CONSULTANT My name is Rick Barrera. Everything I've done for the last twenty-five years has been really focused on bringing the voice and the viewpoint of the customer into organizations.

Rancho Cucamonga, CA

MARKETING COORDINATOR My name is Lindy Williams and I work for Reef Company in San Diego. It's pretty exciting to look at a map and determine where you want to go promote Reef products in the world.

MARKETING DIRECTOR My name is P.J. Connell. I'm the men's marketing director at Reef Company in San Diego. Right now I'm planning a worldwide Reef tour. I also do regional and international WCT tour events.

San Diego, CA

MATERIALS SUPPLIER My name is Zach Kaplan. I'm the CEO of Inventables, a company that collects and shows off new materials and new ideas. Our mission is to build a living showcase of what's possible to deliver inspiration and innovation to the dreamers of the world.

Central Square, NY

MECHANIC My name is Mark Martino. I own Mark's Service Center in Hastings, New York. Our guys fixed the pulley on that Pursue the Passion RV….what an oddball vehicle that is.

MEDICAL CONSULTANT My name is Kathy Murhead. I'm a head for rent. My job is to ask the hard questions. 'How do you know it will do what you think it's going to do? It's like being an aunt or an uncle instead of a parent. You get 80% of the fun and only 20% of the hard work.

Akron, OH

MEDICAL RESEARCHER My name Chris Wooddell. I love my job. Research is really fun. It's like this wild roller coaster ride. If you design an experiment well, you get information. And every little step moves you forward toward the goal.

MOTIVATIONAL SPEAKER My name is Stephen Hopson. I was born deaf. My first job was on Wall Street, and my last job was also on Wall Street. I am the first deaf instrument rated pilot. But I'm still hungry with different goals. I want to have my first book published. I'm hungry to speak around the world.

Portland, OR

MUSCULAR DYSTROPHY ADVOCATE My name is Scott Hatley. I was born with muscular dystrophy. That was part of the inspiration for founding our non profit, Incight. The other part was the effect that we can have on the youth. We now have 70 scholars with disabilities. It will be exciting to have the first couple job placements.

MUSIC PRODUCER My name is Peter Dyson. Until three years ago, I worked for a semiconductor company. I now own Studio West, the biggest recording studio in San Diego. It's a little closer to what I'm passionate about.

San Diego, CA

NAME TAG GUY I'm Scott Ginsberg. I've worn a name tag for 2,491 days straight, and I'm going to wear this thing for the rest of my life. 24/7. I consider myself an entrepreneur. I write books, I give speeches. I do training materials. I have a million things going.

NATURAL BUILDER My name is Bernhard Masterson. I'm a cob builder. I built my house out of cob, and I built the bench we're sitting on out of cob. Building with earth is really environmentally sustainable because you don't have to go very far for the materials. There's plenty of it.

Portland, O

NETWORKING CONSULTANT My name is Melissa Giovagnoli. I'm the President and founder of Networlding. It's founded on the principle that 20 years from now, 99% of the people you know will have a life that's more difficult than they have today. I help them make their life easier through the power of networking.

Chicago, IL

NON PROFIT DIRECTOR My name is Joyce Richards. I'm the President of Junior Achievement in Phoenix. The impact this program is making on kids lives…we're just completely sold on it.

NON PROFIT FOUNDER My name is Phoenix Rowell. I'm the founder of the non profit SMILES Behind Bars. We work to improve the literacy and communication skills of prisoners to increase the chances of them finding employment when they're released.

Orange County, CA

NUTRITIONIST My name is Judy Caplan. I'm a registered dietitian. My company's name is Nutrition Ammunition.

ONLINE DATING ENTREPRENEUR My name is Rachel Begelman. I'm the founder of the online dating site, Econfidant.com. The idea came to me when my friends told me I was great at giving relationship advice.

ORAL HISTORIAN My name is David Rensin. How would I describe my job? Basically, as gainful unemployment. I write books. I interview people. I use that as an excuse to go out and have different experiences in life. My promise to myself in high school was to never have a job, and I've been largely successful.

Chicago, IL

ORGAN EDUCATOR My name is Kathleen Cosart. Six months into my marriage, my husband needed a kidney. I was able to be a donor. My job now at One Legacy is to help do whatever I can to educate people on organ donation.

ORGANIST My name is Gary Pressy. I'm the organist for the Chicago Cubs. It's a great job to have, and fitting for me to have a job like this because I was always a traditionalist. I liked the history of baseball. I get to do the seventh inning stretch with Take Me Out to the Ballgame. What more could you want?

Phoenix, AZ

OUTDOOR ADVERTISER My name is Karl Eller. I'm the namesake of the Eller College of Business down in Tucson at the University of Arizona. I've been in every kind of business you could believe. But from an early age, I've been in love with billboards and the billboard business.

PAELLA GUY My name is Gerard Nebesky. I just do paella. Whoever needs it, wherever. In the islands, New York, SNL, Teri Hatcher's 40th birthday…you name it.

ental, CA

PAINTER I'm Bua. I paint pictures for a living. I have a library in my imagination that I can just pull from. The nice thing about painting is that you're in the now, all the time. It's something that I love and have been doing pretty much my whole life.

Los Angeles, CA

PARK RANGER Name's Ryan Barnes and I'm from North Carolina. I've loved the outdoors since I was born. Always have and always will. Now I'm a park ranger at the primo of all primo places. Old Faithful Yellowstone.

PASSION CATALYST My name is Curt Rosengren. My mission is to help people love their work and change their world in a way that feels personally meaningful to them.

Yellowstone Park, WY

PERSONAL COACH My name is Wanda Marie. I help people find clarity and take action. It's what I do to help heal the planet.

PHARMACEUTICAL SALES REP I'm Eric from Seattle. I'm in Pharmaceutical sales. I get to go around the city and learn about drugs.

PHARMACIST My name is David Martin. I am the director of operations in the pharmacy department at Scottsdale Healthcare. Our job is to get everything right 100% of the time. We decide what is the right drug for the right patient at the right disease state.

Los Angeles, CA

PHOTOGRAPHER My name is Stephen Wayda and I'm one of the luckiest men in the world. I'm a photographer for Playboy.

PHOTOGRAPHER My name is Christopher Barr. The cameras, the lights, all that stuff is really about ten percent of what I do. The other ninety percent is working with people. Understanding where they are and taking them to the place where I need them to be.

PHYSICAL THERAPIST My name is Jeff Abernethy. I'm in the outpatient orthopedics area at Scottsdale Healthcare. I'm not sitting behind a desk and I'm active. I get to interact with people and see the impact I make in their lives.

Tucson, AZ

PHYSICIST My name is Nicolaas Bloembergen. I'm 86. I received the Nobel Prize in Physics when I was 61 for my contribution to the development of laser spectroscopy.

PIPE FITTER My name is Regan. I'm a pipe fitter in Seattle.

PIZZA SHOP OWNER My name is Mark Starr. I'm the owner of David's Pizza in Spokane, Washington next to Gonzaga University. I hate to think of myself as the old fat Italian guy behind the counter with stains all over my apron, but I might be that guy.

Spokane, WA

PLAYBOY PLAYMATE My name is Samantha Harris. I was discovered as a Hawaiian Tropic Girl in Orlando and now I'm Playboy Playmate.

Los Angeles, CA

POSTER SHOP MANAGER My name is Jim Sherraden. I'm the manager and janitor at Hatch Show Print in Nashville, Tennessee. When you look at all the generations of folks who've run the shop, go back to 1879 when Edison invented the light bulb. I'm glad I don't have to give a pitch as to why this shop is special. People seem to figure it out with their own senses.

POUND CAKE PRODUCER My name is Amy Hilliard. I'm the President & CEO of Comfort Cake that's headquartered in Chicago. My daughter created the slogan for our company when she was 14: 'Pound cake so good it feels like a hug.'

Chicago, IL

PR COORDINATOR My name is Marty Maloney. I'm the Public Relations Coordinator with the Chicago White Sox. I grew up on the Southside. To work for a baseball team is unbelievable, but to do it for your hometown team is absolutely amazing.

PR FIRM PARTNER My name is Steve Cody. I'm the co-founder and managing partner of Peppercom, New York's fastest growing public relations firm in 2008. The firm is named after our family dog, Pepper.

Beaverton, OR

PRINTING SALESMAN My name is Tyler Sumrok. I sell print products for Prisma Graphic in Phoenix, Arizona.

PRODUCT DIRECTOR My name is Josiah Lake. I'm the Product Line Manager of Footwear for the Jordan Brand at Nike. My job allows me to see footwear from its design phase to its retail phase. I get to see what people want in a Jordan shoe.

PROFESSIONAL GOLFER My name is Shirley Furlong. I started as a golf professional playing on the LPGA tour. As a playing professional, that was my living. Now I teach the game of golf and help people improve their games.

Chandler, AZ

PUBLIC DEFENDER My name is Kathy Cima. From when I was younger, this is the job I've always wanted. You deal with these very interesting fact sets. I work with kids when they get charged with crimes. That's part of the job. The other part is working with parents when the county comes in and takes their kids away and they want them back. We represent the parents to try to get them back.

PUBLIC RELATIONS PRINCIPAL My name is Gary Springer. I grew up in show business. My dad was a press agent for Bette Davis, Henry Fonda, Joan Crawford…my babysitter was Marilyn Monroe. What can you say? Ain't no business like show business.

New York, NY

PUBLIC RELATIONS STRATEGIST My name is Sandi Serling. I have my own PR firm and I ride motorcycles. The motorcycle is risky, much like self employment. But risk is rewarded with great gain.

PUBLIC RELATIONS STRATEGIST My name is Monica Rohleder. I spent $300 on a career test, and it was the best $300 I ever spent. It got me into PR.

Lake Oswego,

RADIO DJ My name is Emilee Warner. I am the voice of CMT Radio Networks in Nashville, Tennessee. I am 21 years old. I really love great music and I love exposing people to great music.

RADIO JOURNALIST My name is Rene Gutel. I never know from one day to the next who I'm going to interview. I've had the luck to interview politicians, musicians, authors, professors, and so many people from different walks of life. I get to walk up to them with a microphone and ask them any question pertaining to the topic at hand.

Nashville, TN

RAPPER I go by the name of Lucky I Am. I'm an MC. I'm an indie music maker. And a public speaker. I'm the Tony Robbins of the indie world.

REAL ESTATE DEVELOPER My name is Bill Gallagher. As a developer builder, you get to create. You get to find land and draw the plans and get the financing and get the packages together. If you do it well, then you're rewarded well. If you don't, you suffer.

Phoenix, AZ

REAL ESTATE INVESTOR My name is Jesus Delgado. I believe I have the classic American story. Immigrant family escapes to US, son serves country, then moves on to build billion dollar company and becomes a philanthropist.

RECORD STORE OWNER My name is Keith Covart. I'm the owner of Electric Fetus Record Store in Minneapolis. Playing music that you want to play, and that's your job? That's pretty cool. It's better than selling widgets. You can't listen to widgets.

Santa Rosa, C

RECRUITER My name is Lynn Hazan. Recruiting took advantage of my innate curiosity. I love making connections with people on opportunities. If a company chooses to pay me, they want top talent. So I find the best candidate that fits their needs.

REGISTERED NURSE My name is Maggie Slade and I am a RN supervisor on the orthopedic floor. I strongly feel that nurses run the hospital. Without us patients would be in bad shape, and so would the doctors because they need us. I think we're the core of it all.

RELOCATION DIRECTOR My name is Rayne Martin. I manage a department that deals with all the relocation and implementation of social services for the Chicago Housing Authority in the Plan for Transformation. I'm responsible of the movement of 25,000 families through a ten year period.

Minneapolis, N

REPORTER My name is Andrew Hasbun. People will tell you whether they're doing print journalism or broadcast that they've wanted to do it since they were a kid. That's how it was for me. I would watch CNN in 7th grade when everyone else was watching some other junk.

Phoenix, AZ

RESTAURANT CHAIN MANAGER My name is Javier Correa Jr. My dad started Sombrero's Mexican Food back in 1984, when I was 2 years old. I remember growing up and working the cash registers. Now I'm helping him manage 16 locations in San Diego.

RESTAURANT MANAGER My name is Matthias Merges. I've been with Charlie Trotters for 12 years. I'm the executive chef and general manager. I'm the one who runs the ship for Charlie.

San Diego, CA

RETAIL CLOTHING INVESTOR My name is Ronnie Ghenender. I've been in retail for more than 40 years. I'm one of the financial partners for LRG Clothing. It's kind of the American dream to have money work for you instead of you working for money.

ROCKET SCIENTIST My name is Joe Manzo. I'm an aerodynamics engineer at Orbital Sciences Corporation. I deal with supersonic, hypersonic flight. Imcompressible, compressible flow. Invicid, vicid flow. Overflow. CFD++. Complex codes that solve...you might have not followed all that. Basically, I build rockets.

Chicago, IL

SALES DIRECTOR 'This is Jarrod Dillion calling with the Oakland Raiders.' That's what I used to say 60, 70, 80 times a day on the phone. Now I'm responsible for making sure that we're hitting our big macro goals with our season ticket plans as our Director of Ticket Sales.

SALARY ARBITRATOR My name is Matt Klentak. I work in the Commissioner's Office in New York. My job is to advise the 30 major league baseball teams on player signings for arbitration. I help teams spend their money wisely.

New York, NY

SAXOPHONIST My name is Sal Andolina. I've played the sax with the Buffalo Philharmonic Orchestra for the last 17 years and have been lucky enough to play at venues around the world in between.

SCREENWRITER My name is Josh Olson. I'm the screenwriter for History of Violence. I have a license to put myself in the head of all kinds of strange and interesting people and walk around in their shoes for awhile. That, to me, is the best part about the job.

SERIAL ENTREPRENEUR My name is Matt Flannery. My wife and I founded the non-profit Kiva.org after taking a trip to Africa. Kiva connects people through lending for the sake of alleviating poverty.

Buffalo, NY

SKEET SHOOTER Name's Judy. I supervise and train the knuckleheads and skeet shooters that come out to the range. I shoot better than all of 'em.

Atlanta, GA

SKIN CREATOR I'm Kelly Van Winkle from Madison, Wisconsin. I love my job. I work with research and development so we can make skin for burn victims.

SOCIAL ACTIVIST My name is Nicole Sotelo. People often say, 'Oh my voice isn't heard.' But it does make a difference! I'm really trying to help bring women's equality issues to the forefront. Sometimes you have to take it in your own hands to work for justice and see change in the world.

SOFTWARE ENGINEER My name is Lucas Forschler. My official title is software engineer design and test. I'm kind of a gadget freak. I love working for Microsoft, a company that helps create the really cool gadgets. It keeps things interesting.

Chicago, IL

SOFTWARE ENGINEER SUPERVISOR My name is Richard Hamilton. I oversee a team of six programmers who write software for the Microsoft Corporation. I'm also the guy who receives the reports when people choose not to click 'Don't Send' when people have problems online.

SOFTWARE EXECUTIVE I'm Troy Henikoff. I'm President of the Amacai Corporation. My role is to make sure we have a clear direction and make sure everyone understands what the goal is of the team.

Redmond, WA

SOUND DESIGNER My name is Dave Lowmiller. I am the senior sound designer and composer here at Rainbow Stuidos. I get to break stuff. And I don't get in trouble. And I get to put that sound into a video game. I don't know what else to tell ya. I get to create sound design assets and write music and I get paid for it. That's the dream.

SPORTS MARKETER My name is Brandyn Cooper, but everyone calls me 'Coop.' I work with Nike NBA players in all different capacities from going to photo shoots, making sure they have the right shoes to play in, going to games to watch them play, and build relationships with the players so that Nike can service them better.

Phoenix, AZ

STAFF EDITOR My name is Ford Burkhart. I'm a copy editor at the Foreign Desk for the *New York Times*. I'm like the third base coach who waves runners in for the score. I'm the last one to see the stories before they go into the paper.

STAFFING FIRM CEO My name is Tom Gimbel. I own a staffing firm focusing on Accounting & Finance professionals in Chicago

STAGE MANAGER My name is Tom Bartlett. As a stage manager, I get to be the center of the hourglass. Whenever anything comes through the hour glass, whether it's stage issues, actor issues, costume issues, lighting issues, rehearsals, everything filters through the stage manager.

Las Vegas,

STARTUP ENTHUSIAST I'm Andrew Hyde. I love startups. I love making things people use. I love design. I love that things I have created are spreading across the world. I work for TechStars, which is the premiere venue for starting a startup.

Boulder, CO

STARTUPOLOGIST My name is Rich Sloan. I'm the co-founder of the website Startupnation.com, a business advice and networking site for entrepreneurs. I love helping people create businesses that fit their dreams.

STREET ARTIST My name is Ethan Harrington. I paint pictures for a living. That's all I do. I stand outside. I pick different scenes in the city to paint. And I also have a series of paintings of scantily clad young ladies with guns and whiskey. So that's what I do.

Seattle, WA

STUDENT TRAVEL AGENT My name is Meghan Hoover. I'm the founder of XploreU.com, an online student travel community and resource for colleges across America.

SURFER My name is Mike Hynson. Hello, and goodbye.

SUSTAINABILITY ACTIVIST My name is John Powers. I'm the founder of Alliance for Sustainable Colorado. The problems we face are so big that we get people working together to develop policies and implement practices of sustainability.

Chicago, IL

T-SHIRT PROMOTIONS DIRECTOR My name is Bob Nanna and my position at Threadless is I set up all of the special promotions that we do with bands, events, and movies and stuff. That's my main job.

TASTEMASTER My name is Raymond Karam and my job title is Senior Tastemaster at Cold Stone Creamery. Making ice cream products is what I love to do. I eat ice cream every day. In fact, I just had some.

Venice, CA

TATTOO ARTIST My name is Kevin Hinton. I live in Venice. When people ask what I do for a living, I always say I'm a tattoo artist. Some people go, 'Oh,' when I tell them that. Like it's different. But you can buy a painting on the wall. And then you can sell it. Someone buying art from me, forever, on their body is way more of a complement than $50,000 for a black dot.

TEACHER My name is Sabrina Philliplanck. I teach 7th, 8th, 9th, and 11th grade English in Vancouver. I love my job. Watching the kids learn every day is always new and always exciting.

Seattle, WA

TECH ENTREPRENEUR My name is Nathan Kaiser. I'm the founder of the website, nPost.com, a resource for people looking into the world of tech start ups. Many people thought I was crazy to leave a good job to start this, but I'd rather be crazy than working unhappily.

TECHNICAL ARTIST My name is Bryan Moss. I manage the communication between two departments. You have the programmers, and you have the artists. I'm the go between the two. Whatever the other needs, I make sure they get it so we can make video games.

West Chicago, IL

TECHNOLOGY BUSINESS DEVELOPER My name is Eric Olson. I was working in Business Development for Feedburner, but that was acquired a few months ago by Google. So now I have this Google badge and I'm working in Partner Development. I also am one of the co-founders of TECH cocktail.

TELEPHONE REPAIRMAN My name is Christopher Cook. I've been repairing people's telephones for the last 17 years.

Mountain View, CA

THAT GUY My name is Noah Kagan. I hate the question, 'What do you do for a living?' I think it's the worst question. Back in the day I used to say I worked at Walgreen's because I didn't want people judging me. But, if you want to know what I do, I make things happen, eat burritos, and for the most part, kick a whole lot of ass.

THERAPEUTIC HORSE TRAINER My name is Miriam Smith and I run a non profit called Equi-Star, which is a therapeutic horse riding ranch in Burt, New York.

TOUR GUIDE My name is John Condon. I'm a former Sonoma County deputy sheriff turned tour guide. I load groups into my 12 passenger van and cart them to the wineries that have made Sonoma and Napa counties a worldwide destination.

Burt, N

TRAVELING NURSE My name is Geraldine Gleeson McNulty. I'm actually from the South of Ireland. About a 150 miles from Dublin. I love nursing. It's taken me all around the world.

TRAVELING PHOTOGRAPHER My name is Greg Davis. I travel around the world and take pictures. I set up less than two years ago. Big things are happening just by exposing stories from around the world to as many people as I can.

Sonoma County, C

TV HOST My name is Jake Sasseville. How do you give a one line bio on yourself?

VENTURE CAPITALIST My name is Brad Feld. I've been an early stage investor and entrepreneur for over twenty years. I'm the co-founder of the Foundry Group, a venture capital firm focused on investing in early-stage information technology companies.

New York,

VICE PRESIDENT OF SALES My name is Jeff Tucker. I've been with the San Francisco Giants for 15 years now. In sales and in life, you can't be afraid of the word 'no.' The opportunities are out there. You just have to show passion and be persistent.

VIDEO GAME DESIGNER My name is Trey Smith. I design video games at EA Sports. I'm the assistant producer 3…whatever the hell that means.

Vancouver, Canada

VIDEOGRAPHER My name is Scott Foreman. I'm the Director of Post Production at Jobing.com in Phoenix. Video doesn't lie. If you're not passionate about the video you're producing, it's going to reflect in the final product.

VISION ARCHITECT My name is Charles Planck. I'm the CEO and vision architect of Articulated Impact in Washington D.C. Ever since I designed my first Web page in the mid-90's, I've been fascinated with the ways technology can change how we think of value. That potential for change is why I do what I do.

Oakland, CA

VOICEOVER AGENT My name is Hoss. I've helped a number people retire from their day jobs so that they can do voiceover full time. I have a few of those clients, and I call those people my life's work. They are people you have definitely heard on the radio and seen on television.

WARDEN My name is Tom. At 26, I was sentenced to 11 years in a maximum security penitentiary. I'm 74 now, and I'm the first convict to become a warden of a prison.

Niagara Falls, NY

WEDDING PHOTOGRAPHER My name is Laura Dombrowski and I tell stories about life with images. That's what I do.

WINE SALESMAN My name is Stewart Bryan. What I do is I'm involved in the sales and marketing of our product. The fun thing is establishing a relationship with a buyer and selling this romantic item. You do things that sort of take on a personal relationship.

Sonoma County, CA

WORKFORCE CONSULTANT My name is Tammy Erickson. I've spent my whole career in consulting. I've always been in a situation of working with different companies on different issues at different points in time.

WRITER My name is Mary Jane Grinstead. I was in line to compete for the CEO's job at a half a billion dollar startup when I decided to quit my job to become a writer. I do some freelance business writing, and am working on finding a publisher for a fiction book.

YOGA MASTER My name is Daren Freisen. I'm the owner of Moksha Yoga Studios in Chicago. I've had a couple reincarnations in this life. I've had the corporate job. I did some work for the White House. I'm on a completely different path now. One of my Kharmic dispositions is to help people. Here at the yoga studio, this is a way I can do that.

Chicago, IL

YOUTH ORGANIZATION CEO My name is Tommy Spaulding. Twenty years after traveling the world with Up With People, I'm the CEO of the organization. If we're going to build a great America, it's really about building an America of ownership, where community service is what you do when you do something right.

YOUTH PROGRAM DIRECTOR My name is Dan Isherwood and this is my business partner Jim Dower. Together, we formed Urban Initiatives, which is a health and education soccer program. We provide programs to 1st- 4th graders in six different schools in Chicago.

Phoenix, AZ

ZOO DIRECTOR My name is Dan Subaitis. I oversee the entire living collection here at the Phoenix Zoo. Everything that's an animal and plants. And everyone that takes care of those animals and plants. I'm one of those lucky people that enjoy what I do for a living. The older you get, the more you realize how rare that is.

BRETT FARMILOE My name is Brett Farmiloe. I'm the author/editor of this book. Everyone always asks me the question, 'What have you learned?' As you can imagine, that's a pretty tough question to answer. What I've learned from the people featured in 'Roll the Credits' formed the foundation of what I believe in today. What I learned by living in an RV with these three guys taught me a lot about people, and taught me a lot about myself. And last but not least, I've learned that when you pursue a passion, you end up in places you never could have foreseen. It's incredibly gratifying to go the route described in this book, and I believe it's the only way to live.

I have a lot of people to thank- sponsors, hosts, interviewees, supporters, everyone who helped make Pursue the Passion happen- without you none of this would have been possible. I'd also like to thank you for reading this book. I hope the message was clear, and that it left an impact. Feel free to reach out to me anytime if you'd like: brett@pursuethepassion.com, @thatpassionguy, facebook.com/brettfarmiloe.

JAY WHITING What's up everybody? I'm Jay Whiting. I got on board with Pursue the Passion because I believed in what Brett was trying to do and knew that we could make it happen if we worked together. I saw our trip as a once in a lifetime opportunity to do something for the greater good, improve myself and make some friends, all while spreading my music across the country. The trip was truly transformational for me. I'd like to thank every single person that we met on our journey. It would not have been the same experience without each and every one of your stories, guidance, warmth, generosity, friendship and of course, couches.

Today, I work for Jobing.com as a videographer in Los Angeles. When I'm not shooting and editing fresh recruitment videos, you can find me at the Mysterious Mammal recording studio working on my music or hanging out with my family. It

doesn't leave much time for sleep, but you gotta do what you gotta do for the things you want out of this life. My group, Class Project (myspace.com/classproject), will be dropping the "Ably Illegitimate" Mixtape in late 2009 and our sophomore album, "The Audacity of Dope" in the Spring of 2010. Also look out for my forth-coming solo project entitled, "Genre, Shmenre" under the alias: J. Foxx. I am exactly where I want/need/hoped to always be. I am truly blessed.

NOAH POLLOCK My name is Noah Pollock and I joined Pursue the Passion because I didn't know what I wanted to do with my life. Being on the road and writing for the site was my favorite experience of my 25 years on this planet. While I am still not entirely sure about the life plan, I am currently the Senior Creative Writer at Vision Design Studio in Long Beach, CA, living happily with my cat/spiritual advisor Elbea.

ZACH HUBBELL My name is Zach Hubbell and I was the last lucky addition to the Pursue the Passion Tour. To me the trip represented inspiration and opportunity when I needed it most. I had tried what I knew and found that what I thought I should be doing wasn't leading me in a direction I wanted to go. Pursue the Passion was the greatest learning experience I've ever had and the best time of my life. Four buddies, traveling the country, talking to strangers about what mattered most to them. It changed the way I look at the world.

Thanks to everyone who we met along the way and gave a part of themselves to our project. Since the trip ended I've continued to work with Brett on Pursue the Passion; filming interviews, working with students and speaking about our experience. Brett's done a great job on the book and I think it's important that the stories are available to others. Currently I'm the Social Media Manager for Jobing.com. I'm building something new and helping people find work that inspires them. Life is good.